BEYOND

loneliness

BEYOND
loneliness

THE GIFT OF
GOD'S FRIENDSHIP

—————

TREVOR HUDSON

UPPER
ROOM BOOKS®
NASHVILLE

Cover design: Jeff Miller | Faceout Studio
Cover photo: Victor Bezrukov
Interior design and typesetting: Kristin Goble | PerfecType

Library of Congress Cataloging-in-Publication Data

Names: Hudson, Trevor, 1951–
Title: Beyond loneliness : the gift of God's friendship / Trevor Hudson.
Other titles: Friendship with God.
Description: Nashville : Upper Room Books, [2016] | Originally published:
    Friendship with God. South Africa : Struik Christian Books, 2014.
Identifiers: LCCN 2015032549| ISBN 9780835815192 (print) |
    ISBN 9780835815314
    (mobi) | ISBN 9780835815208 (epub)
Subjects: LCSH: Spirituality—Christianity. | Friendship—Religious
    aspects—Christianity.
Classification: LCC BV4501.3 .H821844 2016 | DDC 231.7—dc23
LC record available at http://lccn.loc.gov/2015032549

For Dallas Willard (1935–2013), whose joyful life, radiant witness, and faithful friendship gave me a glimpse of what it really means to live as God's friend.

For William A. Barry, SJ, whose many writings have guided and helped me in deepening my own friendship with God.

CONTENTS

ACKNOWLEDGMENTS

To Joanna Bradley, Jeannie Crawford-Lee, and the publishing and marketing teams at Upper Room Books—thank you for your constant encouragement and support in the ministry of writing. I learn a great deal from your editing process.

To Gary Moon, dear friend and ministry colleague at the Dallas Willard Center at Westmont College—thank you for your trust in me and for writing such a generous and grace-filled foreword.

To a number of the finest friends a person could have—thank you for praying for me throughout this writing journey and for continuously helping me believe that I have something worthwhile to share.

To the colleagues and members of Northfield Methodist Church in Benoni and Mosaiek in Johannesburg, South Africa—thank you for sharing together in the friendship and life that God makes possible for us.

To William A. Barry, SJ, Annemarie Paulin-Campbell, Johan Geyser, Mags Blackie, Russell Pollitt, SJ, and Nathan Foster—thank you for your willingness to read and offer your comments on the book.

And most of all, to Debbie, my closest friend, and to my children, Joni and Mark, together with their marriage partners, James and Marike—thank you for the lightness and joy and color each of you brings into my life.

FOREWORD

F riendship—what an amazing gift! Friendship is being in a relationship with another person in which you both feel deep affec-
tion, empathy, compassion, selflessness, and trust. It's when you
greatly enjoy the company a friend and are free to express any feeling. You can relax into being yourself—warts and all—knowing that
your friend has your best interest at heart. You can confess mistakes
without any fear of judgment or that the story will be repeated. And
a friend never checks to see what time it is when you are talking.
Friendship is a nice invention.

Trevor Hudson makes a bold claim in this book: Part of the good
news of the gospel is that we are invited into a friendship with God.
If Trevor were not my friend, I'm not sure I'd believe him.

I became acquainted with Trevor Hudson many years ago. I had
written my first book, *Homesick for Eden*. It had been out a few
months, and I had begun to wonder if anyone had actually read it
besides my mother. Then one morning in the copy room of the gradu-
ate school where I taught, coffee in one hand, fingering through the
contents of my mailbox with the other, I came across a small envelope
with a South African postmark. I quickly opened the letter and found
a handwritten note from Trevor, in which he expressed his appreciation for my book and made a positive reference to two people for
whom I had great respect—Dallas Willard and Leslie Weatherhead.

On my second reading of the note I saw that Trevor was planning a trip to the United States and would be in Atlanta, Georgia.

He wondered if we might get together. While he had me at "I liked the book," the fact that he knew Dallas Willard and enjoyed reading Leslie Weatherhead was overwhelming proof that I would enjoy meeting this man from South Africa who had such excellent taste in literature.

It has been almost two decades since Trevor showed up in Atlanta. He was able to stay for part of two days—enough time to make it possible for him to ride to my home far out into the country and spend time with my wife and two daughters. Trevor was an instant hit with the family.

During those days, I learned that Trevor had invited Dallas Willard to travel to South Africa with only the promise of a sofa to sleep on and a small crowd of ministers (on one visit, they fit around one table) to speak to—and that Dallas said yes, for that and multiple other visits. I learned about his love for his wife and two children, his work as a Methodist minister during the most difficult times in South Africa, the fact that he had done jail time with Desmond Tutu, and that he was a pretty good table tennis player, even though we still disagree about who won the majority of the games. In short, Trevor and I became friends, and I began to look for ways to work together on projects.

And it turns out that finding projects to complete together was not a great difficulty. Trevor not only "gets" Dallas Willard, but also he is one of the few people I know who can teach Dallas's key ideas about Christian spiritual formation in a way that is accurate, engaging, and right from the heart. He does so with story, rich examples from family life, and always with a South African accent—which is the same way he writes. When Dallas was no longer able to teach in the Renovaré Institute, Trevor stepped in to do much of the teaching and he, like Dallas, is greatly loved and appreciated by the students.

Trevor has written many fine books, but I believe this one is my favorite. In it he takes one of Jesus' greatest offers—to call his followers friends—and helps the reader find the path from loneliness to intimacy with God. Trevor tells us that God desires our friendship, and he is not alone in making this claim. As you will discover, he shares from experiences of over four decades of savoring insights from the first Christian book he read, Leslie Weatherhead's *The Transforming Friendship: A Book About Jesus and Ourselves*. And he also draws on Dallas Willard's insights, which have seeped into Trevor's soul through time and close relationship. In Dallas Willard's first book (originally titled *In Search of Guidance* but now titled *Hearing God*), he describes a developing relationship with God that progresses through the stages of conversation, communion, and union—not unlike a romantic relationship.

Trevor is also an Ignatian scholar. In this book you will find beautiful reflections on the way people think about friendship—which can, in turn, give new life to how you view your relationship with God. In the words of James Martin, SJ, in *The Jesuit Guide to (Almost) Everything: A Spirituality for Real Life*, "If we look at what makes a healthy friendship, we'll see that some of the same traits help make for a good relationship with God."[1]

Another notable, modern-day Jesuit, William A. Barry, SJ, observed in his wonderful little book *God and You: Prayer as a Personal Relationship* that there are many exciting parallels between developing personal friendships and developing a deep and authentic relationship with God. According to James Martin's distillation of insights from Barry, friendships with others and with God should involve the following six elements: (1) spending time together, (2) learning about the other, (3) being honest and transparent, (4) learning to be a good listener, (5) allowing for changing and maturing views of the other, and (6) learning how to enjoy being silent together.

As Trevor says, most of us become aware of a friendship-shaped hole in our lives. In part, this is to be filled by others, but part of this chasm that can only be occupied by God.

God has given us a beautiful story about the character of God through the life of Jesus. Jesus makes friends. We see his deep love for Mary, Martha, and Lazarus and the empathetic tears he weeps when Lazarus dies—even though he knows the story will have a happy ending. We see him desiring the company of Peter, James, and John when he is in pain and when he has amazing things to share. And we see in John 15:15 that Jesus changes the identity of the twelve disciples from servants to friends.

Would you like to become God's friend? If so, the book in your hands is a wonderful place to begin. You will love the warm and approachable language of the author, appreciate his wisdom born from forty years of pastoral experience, and enjoy the well-organized chapters. You will find the practical exercises that Trevor provides to be excellent ways to experience a transforming friendship with the Trinity. As Dallas Willard was so fond of pointing out, the words in John 17:3 are the only ones Jesus offers as a definition of eternal life:"Now this is eternal life: that they know you, the only true God, and Jesus Christ, whom you have sent" (NIV).

Beyond Loneliness is a wonderful book about two interwoven themes—friendship with God and personal transformation. It is a guidebook for stepping into the eternal living described and modeled by Jesus.

—Gary W. Moon, MDiv, PhD
Executive Director of the Martin Institute
and Dallas Willard Center, Westmont College
Author of *Apprenticeship with Jesus:
Learning to Live Like the Master*

AN INVITATION TO
TRANSFORMING FRIENDSHIP

L oneliness touches each one of us. None of us escapes it completely. Loneliness is no respecter of age or rank. Whether a young
student, a stay-at-home mom, a busy executive, a retired pensioner, a
grieving widower or widow, or even a pastor working with people every
day, we all know what it means to be lonely. Loneliness may be one of
the most painful experiences that we go through in this life. Perhaps
we find ourselves living in the midst of it at this very moment.

Strikingly, many people who live alone never feel lonely, yet some
who live with others in crowded cities know only too acutely how
loneliness can infect our lives. When we think of loneliness we often
visualize the aged who live alone, but a young adult moving to a new
city, an entrepreneur beginning a business, a partner in a struggling
marriage, or a leader in a challenging corporate environment can be
as lonely as a solitary elderly person in a one-room apartment.

Only genuine and real friendship with God and others can transform loneliness. Perhaps this is why the first Christian book I ever
read made such an impact on me. Soon after I started following
Christ at the age of sixteen, a friend gave me a book. I read it over and
over, savoring its many insights for my new life of faith. The other day
I took it off my library shelf and looked through it again. Its title still
speaks to me of the essential gifts of the Christian faith. The book,
written by British Methodist minister Leslie Weatherhead, is titled
The Transforming Friendship: A Book About Jesus and Ourselves.

Weatherhead's title emphasizes two important dimensions of our experience with God. First, it presents friendship as a helpful analogy for the intimate kind of relationship God wants with us. Put simply, the gospel invites us into friendship with God. This is a staggering reality. The Creator God who loves us, who spoke the whole universe into existence, and who sustains our lives in the immediacy of each moment wants our intimate friendship. Absolutely mind-blowing! I hope that as we explore this good news together, we will be encouraged to see our faith and our lives in totally new ways.

Second, Weatherhead's title clearly states that friendship with God transforms us. Learning to trust God as our Divine Friend has a transforming effect on every aspect of our lives. It affects how we pray, our relationships with others, and the way we understand our everyday existence. Trusting God as our Divine Friend changes the way we think and feel, what we desire and long for, the way we see each other, and how we seek to live in the world. Our friendship with God creates the environment in which we become the people God wants us to be.

In this book I explore these two interwoven themes of friendship and personal transformation. I have been engaging these themes for many years in pastoral conversations, spiritual direction, retreat settings, sermons, lectures, and conferences, and I am continually struck by people's positive response. They often find themselves strongly drawn to the possibility of growing a friendship with God and the ways this could change their lives for the better. I believe that the gospel idea of a transforming friendship with God is one whose time has come. Let's discuss why I believe this to be true.

The Pull of Friendship

First, I have noticed that people resonate with the idea of God's transforming friendship because the concept of friendship is easy to grasp. Most people know what a friend is. A friend is someone we appreciate, someone we enjoy spending time with, someone we are glad to see. Moreover, a friend is someone we trust, someone we commit ourselves to in some way. He or she is someone with whom we find ourselves sharing who we are, sharing stories and ideas we might not share with everyone. A friend is also someone whom we want to serve and help. These experiences of human friendship give us an accessible way of talking about what a relationship with God involves.

Second, God's transforming friendship excites our interest because we know how human friendships change us. For example, we may value one of our friend's qualities, and it begins to rub off on us. Or our friend says something that really hits home, and it turns our thinking upside down. Or a friend poses a difficult question no one else would risk asking that leads to discoveries about ourselves we otherwise would not have made. When friends get together, they mutually influence each other. If this takes place so naturally in human friendships, think of how much more our friendship with God can change the way we think and live.

Third, God's transforming friendship is invitational and promises an unfolding journey. Friendships do not mature overnight. They take time to grow as two people share together, listen to each other's life stories, and slowly move into each other's worlds. The same progression is true of our relationship with God. God does not force all of God's self onto us at once, and we do not give all of ourselves to God at once either. The adventure of forming a friendship with God takes a lifetime of walking with God. Rather than putting people off, I have found that this possibility draws people powerfully into the pilgrimage of personal growth and development.

Fourth, the prospect of a transforming friendship with God attracts people who are frustrated with cold religion, impersonal churches, and anonymous worship experiences that can intensify loneliness. An answer to the problem of loneliness in our Christian faith can be found as long as we help one another to experience genuine friendship with God and with others along the way. Often these two experiences go hand in hand. Telling a lonely person that God is his or her friend can sound very hollow. It only becomes meaningful when we make the divine friendship real by modeling it in our own relationships.

Lastly, forty years as a pastor has shown me that a friendship-shaped hole exists in all our lives. Loneliness is a painful experience because we are created with a longing for intimacy, connection, and relationship. Most people intuitively understand that there is a longing within them; yet, others resist the longing. When we hear about God's offer of transforming friendship, I hope we will recognize it as what we are really looking for so that we can explore it further. I believe that if we experience such a relationship, our deepest loneliness may be healed.

What About You?

Consider the following questions:

- Do you feel lonely?
- Is there a friendship-shaped hole in your life?
- Are you open to reimagining your relationship with God as a friendship?
- Do you want to be transformed into the person God wants you to be?
- Does the possibility of starting a lifelong journey with God attract you?
- Do you long for a real experience of the living God?

If you answered yes to any of these questions, join me in discovering how to begin a transforming friendship with God.

Friends of God Transform the World

Sometimes people ask me whether pursuing friendship with God makes our faith journey too private, irrelevant to the suffering of people around us, or unrelated to the struggles taking place on our streets. I believe the opposite to be true. When we enter into the Divine Friendship, we are drawn into God's greater dream for the healing of our lonely and broken world. We are created to become friends of God and to partner with God in making God's dream a reality in the world.

Again, I believe God's friendship is something for which our hearts intuitively long. For the past few years, I've written a nightly prayer on Twitter. The other evening I tweeted the following prayer: *Lord, help us to realize that implied in our friendship with you is the call to partner with you to make your dream real here and now.* I was quite taken by the response that prayer generated. Many people know that our true and genuine happiness lies in living in tune with God's dream for our world. We want to make this world a better place, and we were created for that purpose.

Friendship Exercises

As shown by the content of my other books, I am convinced of the importance of action. Information alone seldom transforms lives. While the right information undergirds good living, it is critical that we act on the basis of what we know.

I have included *Friendship Exercises* throughout this book. I hope you will read and reflect on them, either on your own or with others in a small group. Friendships take effort and energy. If this is true for human friendships, it is equally true when it comes to a friendship with God.

I can almost hear your questions. (I have a friend who writes *YBH* in the margins of books, meaning "Yes, but how?") How does friendship with God begin? How do I get to know God as my Divine Friend? How does this Divine Friendship grow? How will God transform me through this friendship? How will friendship with God make me feel less lonely? How do I become part of God's dream for the world? How do I relate to God's other friends? How can God's friendship help me live beyond fear? How do I find out what my Friend wants? How will this friendship with God help me when I suffer?

These are not just your questions; this book wrestles with those concerns. I hope that as you engage in these questions with me, the following pages will shed light on them. And my biggest hope is that your exploration will encourage you to live in friendship with God.

1

Living beyond Loneliness

If Jesus were to walk the streets of our cities and towns today, I can imagine him saying, "Come to me, all who are lonely, and I will give you friendship." How would we respond to an offer like this coming from Jesus? Perhaps at first we would be a bit surprised, maybe even startled. Many people believe that Jesus is far more interested in sorting out the sin in our messed-up lives than in sharing in a simple friendship with us. For a long time I thought that way. But I think very differently today. I now believe that Jesus wants to meet us in our loneliness.

None of us is a stranger to loneliness. We experience this particular ache in our hearts at some stage of our lives. Whether we are young or old, rich or poor, married or single, we have a story to tell about being lonely. Loneliness haunts the lives of those who live in the suburbs and the inner cities, in retirement homes and the new housing developments, in university residences and working-class neighborhoods. It is, as Mother Teresa once wisely observed, the leprosy of our contemporary world.

Yet loneliness is not a topic we easily talk about. We don't want to say aloud, "I feel lonely." We don't want to acknowledge our loneliness, and we are ashamed of it when we do. Instead we will try anything to avoid loneliness. We willingly exchange it for destructive behaviors like bad company, alcohol and drug abuse, casual sex, and unfulfilling relationships. Anything, we sometimes think, is better than admitting we experience the painful ache of loneliness.

But not facing our loneliness comes at a price. As we will see, avoidance brings many dangerous and damaging side effects. Failing to admit our loneliness can wreak havoc in our lives. Indeed, denying it often makes the pain worse. Alternatively, when we recognize it and speak about it with others, our loneliness has the potential to become a creative force for growth and maturity. Loneliness is God's powerful way of drawing us into friendship with God and one another.

Let's look first at the many different faces of loneliness. In doing so we will begin to recognize our particular loneliness, and we will be encouraged to break the silence surrounding it. Only when we have confronted the reality of our loneliness can we grasp the overwhelming significance of what Jesus offers us: transforming friendship with God.

The Different Faces of Loneliness

Too often we associate loneliness with those who are single, those who are isolated, and those who live alone. Nothing could be further from the truth. There is a big difference between being alone and being lonely. Being alone is simply the state of not having others around us. Loneliness, on the other hand, comes mostly when we are disconnected from others in such a way that we feel ignored, overlooked, or not known as we really are. It is the painful ache in our hearts for intimate connection, belonging, and companionship.

Here are four glimpses into the ways loneliness invades our every-day lives.

The Loneliness of Leadership Responsibility

The autobiography of Alex Ferguson, retired manager of the famous Manchester United soccer club in England, made an impression on me. Ferguson is a man admired by millions the world over for his unrivaled success. He is happily married and has spent most of his adult life working alongside others toward common goals. We would not expect him to be someone who experiences loneliness. Yet his reflections on what it means to manage a top soccer club reveal the loneliness that sometimes accompanies the overwhelming responsibilities of being a leader. He states the following:

> But there is a fear of failure in a manager the whole time, and you are on your own a lot. Sometimes you would give anything not to be alone with your thoughts. There would be days when I would be in my office, in the afternoon, and no one would knock on my door because they assumed I was busy. Sometimes I'd hope for that rap on the door. . . . In management you have to face that isolation. You need contact. But they think you're busy with important business and don't want to go near you.[1]

The Loneliness of Superficial Relationships

We've probably all experienced feeling lonely even when we are in a large group of people. It can happen in the places where we work, where we worship, where we party, and even in our own homes. We are not physically alone. We are in the company of others, but our interactions feel empty and superficial. This phenomenon occurs in many marriages. Often celebrities are described as lonely people. They are surrounded by hundreds of adoring fans, but they feel lonely because no one truly knows them.

We may be tempted to think that social media, where new "friends" are only a click away on Facebook and Twitter, can ease this loneliness. For some people this may be the case. But I have learned that these Internet conversations frequently lead to superficial relationships. A friend of mine posted this status update on Facebook: "Really struggling at the moment." In spite of having hundreds of "friends," no one made personal contact with him. Only two asked online if they could pray for him. Sometimes our Internet connections make our loneliness worse.

The Loneliness of Depression

Whether we get depressed because of a biological predisposition, a physiological imbalance, overwhelming life circumstances, or a painfully wounded heart, depression can cause feelings of loneliness. Dark and morbid thoughts fill our minds, making us want to drop out of life or die. The constant tiredness and lack of energy and interest that accompany depression rob us of our zest for life. People stay away from us because they don't know what to say, or they make glib comments like, "It's time for you to pull yourself together." Not surprisingly, along with the depression, a terrible loneliness creeps into our whole sense of being.

Even good friends may fail us in these moments. They may think they are being helpful, but we know they are not. Recently I read Parker Palmer's ruthlessly honest account of his own struggle with depression in his book *Let Your Life Speak: Listening for the Voice of Vocation*. He describes how his depression caused him to feel totally blocked off from his friends, especially those who kept sharing "nice thoughts" with him. He was lonely, terribly lonely, and locked up in the pain of his depression. But one person whom he valued immensely came to massage Palmer's feet for half an hour each day without saying much. Palmer recounts the encouragement he experienced one day when the friend simply said, "It feels like you are getting stronger."[2]

The Loneliness of Loss

When I attended Rhodes University in Grahamstown, South Africa, to study for the pastoral ministry, I also attended lectures in the Department of Social Work. One lecturer was a wonderful woman by the name of Professor LeGrange. One day after a lecture, she drew me aside and said, "Trevor, if you want to be a good pastor, you need to spend the rest of your life seeking to understand the experience of loss." I have never forgotten those words. They will forever influence the shape of my ministry.

We experience loss constantly—the loss of innocence through childhood abuse, the loss of trust through betrayal, the loss of health through sickness, the loss of confidence in ourselves through failure, the loss of marriage through divorce, the loss of familiar surroundings through exile, the loss of a loved one through death, and the list goes on. The painful ache of loneliness often accompanies these losses. Recently I had lunch with an elderly man whose wife died a year ago. He said to me, "You will never know how terrible loneliness can be until you lose the love of your life."

Loneliness without a Face

I find it more difficult to describe this last type of loneliness, which is why I didn't include it in the four faces of loneliness. Even though it may be part of the landscapes of loneliness described above, we sometimes encounter this particular loneliness when everything is going relatively well for us. The four faces of loneliness I have pointed to are responses to external, physical, or emotional situations. This last type is one we experience as we come into this world and as we leave it. This loneliness is an essential part of what it means to be human. Moreover, no other human being has the capacity to heal it effectively, no matter how much he or she may love us or seek to be there for us. I call it "loneliness without a face."

Dallas Willard, a dear friend and mentor, hinted at this basic spiritual loneliness when he reflected on the birth of his first child. He wrote this:

> I painfully realized that this incredibly beautiful little creature we had brought into the world was utterly separate from me and that there was nothing *I* could do that would shelter him from his aloneness before time, brutal events, the meanness of other human beings, his own wrong choices, the decay of his own body and, finally, death.[3]

I can certainly identify with Willard's feelings when I think of my relationships with loved ones. For example, my daughter, Joni, was engaged to be married. Three months before her wedding date, she went cycling with her fiancé. Before they set out, they prayed together. Five minutes later she hit a pothole and flew through her handlebars, crashing onto the ground. When I arrived at the hospital and saw her lying in her bed, her badly injured face bloodied and cut, I knew she would not be able to move forward with her wedding plans. During her year of gradual recovery, with all its struggles and disappointments, I tried to be there for her and with her. But I always knew that in the depths of her heart an incurable loneliness resided that neither I, her mother, her brother, her fiancé, nor any other person could ever take away. She had to go there herself.

When I read the above paragraph to Joni to ask her permission to include it in the book, she simply said, "Dad, you get me." As a young woman in her late twenties, she was already able to identify the painful ache of this loneliness without a face. Surrounded by people who loved her deeply, she still experienced the disappointment and difficulty of the loneliness that no other human being can heal or take away. She discovered that no amount of human love could ever eliminate this loneliness in her soul.

friendship exercise

Perhaps you have known this loneliness without a face in your own life. Consider the following questions:

- Do you often feel as if something is missing in your life, even when things are going well and you have everything you need?
- Recall any moments when you have been overcome by the sheer awe and wonder of this world. At those times did you find yourself reaching for more even if you were uncertain what that "more" was?
- Is your heart sometimes restless, searching, and unsatisfied in its longings?
- Do you ever yearn for someone to fully know, understand, and accept you just as you are?
- In moments of suffering or struggle, in spite of the presence of loved ones, have you ever felt alone?

If you answered yes to any of these questions, you have sensed this loneliness without a face. I want to focus on this loneliness to see where it leads. Some of the wisest people in history have followed this trail, and it has led them into what they consider to be the deepest understanding of their lives.

The Treasure within Our Loneliness

Hidden within our loneliness without a face lies a treasure: the longing that God placed in our hearts for divine friendship. We were created with the purpose of befriending God. Our infinite longings remind us that we are made for the Infinite. We were divinely designed for divine connection. Because this is how we have been wired, the only thing that ultimately will bring us joy and happiness is to know a close friendship with God. It is as if God says to us, "I have placed eternity in your hearts" (Eccles. 3:11, AP). Deep within us there is a hole that only God's living presence can fill.

Foolishly, we continue searching for that something that can fill the God-shaped hole in our lives. We ponder a long list of substitutes. We stuff our lives with food and drink; we stay busy at work; we get hooked on TV shows; we become obsessive sport fanatics; we buy more and more things; we experience one casual sexual encounter after another; we hope that more money will stave off the pain of our unfulfilled longings. But these compulsive activities leave us more unhappy and dissatisfied than ever.

Trying to satisfy our innate longing for God with a substitute leads us toward addiction. In my conversations with recovering alcoholics, I hear them reflect on their drinking days and the reasons for their drinking. One comment I hear most often goes like this: "Trevor, I drank so heavily because it gave me a sense of belonging, even if it was false. When I drank I felt connected to things. I wasn't on my own anymore. I belonged." The experience behind this kind of explanation suggests why the solution to alcoholism—and other forms of addiction—is so often a spiritual one.

Though we recognize our longing for God as the treasure hidden in our loneliness, we cannot diminish the importance of our relationships with people. As we will see later, the divine friendship enhances our friendships with one another. And human friendships have the potential to make God's friendship with us more real. They also help us to deal creatively with those other faces of loneliness named earlier: the loneliness of leadership, the loneliness of depression, the loneliness of superficial relationships, and the loneliness of loss. Still, human friendships possess limitations in that by themselves they cannot fill the friendship-hole that can be filled only by God. No amount of human love can ever satisfy the other loneliness tugging away at our souls.

Only God can bring the loving companionship for which we so desperately yearn into our lives to face that deeper loneliness. Those who consciously enter into divine friendship find that God alone can be with them in such an intimate way that they will seldom experience that profound loneliness again. Perhaps this is what

Jesus means when he says to his disciples at the end of his life, "Remember, I am with you always, to the end of the age" (Matt. 28:20). But let's not jump ahead of ourselves. We will soon discover more about this transforming friendship with God.

Facing Our Loneliness

Here are two more important truths about that painful ache of loneliness: We need to face it, and we need to talk about it. Easier said than done, right? Confessing our loneliness can be incredibly difficult because loneliness has a stigma attached to it. Owning up to our loneliness makes us feel as if something is wrong with us. It feels like we are looking for sympathy or, perhaps worse, attention. It may suggest we have no friends or that we are not good friends ourselves. It can leave us feeling vulnerable, weak, and needy. So we are reluctant to admit our loneliness to ourselves, let alone share it with others. But this silence can be extremely harmful.

What happens when we keep our loneliness to ourselves? We are more likely to make bad choices, especially with regard to where we look for friendship and company. We start to seek solutions in destructive activities such as viewing pornography or drinking alcohol or mindless shopping. Keeping our loneliness to ourselves shuts the doors of our hearts to the possible care and concern of others. By pretending to be what we are not, we keep our relationships on a superficial level. We may also harden our own hearts to the loneliness of others. The list of damaging consequences goes on and on.

On the other hand, when we willingly admit that we are lonely, good things can happen. Certainly we start to live more authentic, honest, and transparent lives. We may discover people around us who are genuinely interested in forming friendships. Our loneliness can become a source for fresh creativity in our work. It may encourage a fresh commitment to serve others. It may help us become more empathetic and understanding in our dealings with people. Perhaps, most critically of all, acknowledging our loneliness can lead us toward acknowledging our innate longing for God.

friendship exercise

I invite you to admit your loneliness, if not to others then to yourself. Answer the following questions:

- What memories of loneliness do you have?
- When have you felt most disconnected from others?
- How have you experienced that painful ache for intimate connection, belonging, and friendship?
- How have you experienced loneliness without a face?

Make a note of those memories and experiences that come to your mind as you consider these questions and write them down on a piece of paper.

How was that exercise? Maybe you remembered a time as a child when you played games by yourself. Or when you were away from home at boarding school, camp, or college. Or when you had to make a major decision that would have far-reaching effects for your future. Or when you went through a difficult time in your marriage and could not speak about it to anyone. Or when you found yourself in great financial difficulty and did not know how you were going to provide for your family. Or when you carried the secret of a shameful action. Or when you lost someone you loved very much. Perhaps, even right now, you are going through one of these experiences and saying to yourself, _I am very lonely._

Admitting our loneliness, whether it has a face or not, can be liberating, hopeful, and life-giving. That's why I encourage others to face their loneliness and to be honest with themselves. At the beginning of this chapter, we imagined Jesus walking the streets where we live and saying, "Come to me, all you who are lonely, and I will give you friendship." In the next chapter we will explore why this offer lies at the heart of the Christian faith.

2

God's Passionate Longing for Friendship

Right where we are this moment, in the midst of whatever loneliness we may be facing, God meets us and holds out a hand of friendship. At the heart of the Christian faith lies an extravagant, grace-filled, and mind-blowing offer. God passionately longs to be friends with us. This is what Jesus, through his life, death, resurrection, and ascended presence throughout the universe, makes possible for every human being. All he asks is that we accept the offer of divine friendship.

Ever since reading my first Christian book, *The Transforming Friendship*, I've used the idea of friendship to imagine my relationship with God. Many people speak of having a "personal relationship" with God. The language of friendship clarifies the kind of relationship God wants. It is not the cold, formal, and sometimes fear-filled relationship between master and servant, boss and employee, owner and slave. Rather, God wants a relationship of close connection, deep belonging, and mutual partnership. Or, in one simple word, *friendship*.

We may find this hard to believe. Some of us have grown up with a picture of God that makes it difficult to imagine God's passionate longing for our friendship. Deep down we feel that God stands against us, is disgusted with us, or is angry with us. Recently, I visited a man battling cancer in the hospital. As I sat down beside him, he said, "I must have done something terribly wrong for God to give me this illness." Unless his present understanding of God changes radically, how will this man experience a trusting and confident friendship with God?

William A. Barry, SJ, one of my favorite writers, says that we all tend to have our own "default" picture of God.[1] This is not an image we describe when others ask us what we believe about God. Rather it is our automatic thought about God when things go wrong, when life crashes around us, when circumstances turn out differently than we want them to. In these crunch times do we still honestly believe that God is with and for us? Or do we resort to a default picture of an angry God punishing us or acting coldly indifferent? We need to be ruthlessly truthful with ourselves about this fundamental understanding of God if we want to experience divine friendship.

Thankfully, we can change our negative default image of God. One way is to live into some of the biblical images and stories that reveal God's desire for intimate connection with us. As we look at some of these passages, we can ask the Holy Spirit to use them as vehicles for experiencing God's intense yearning to befriend us. We can pray, *God, as I meditate now on these scriptures, help me to know your passionate longing for friendship.*

Created for Divine Friendship

The first creation story in Genesis introduces us to the God who lavishly creates our universe and everything in it. (See Genesis 1:1–2:3.) In one part of this story God says, "Let us make humankind in

our image, according to our likeness. . . . So God created humankind in his image, in the image of God he created them; male and
female he created them" (Gen. 1:26-27). Now I'm sure we have
heard these words before. Sadly, familiarity sometimes dulls our
minds to words' staggering implications. I remember clearly the
moment when my own familiarity was pierced by a comment that I
have never forgotten.

On a cold winter's night in South Africa in June 1979, I was
a young pastor working in Boksburg, and my congregation invited
Archbishop Desmond Tutu to spend four Wednesday nights with
us and explore the two creation stories in the book of Genesis. He
related the explosive themes of these opening chapters from the
Bible to our life and witness in apartheid South Africa. It was an
unforgettable experience. On our first night together, Archbishop
Tutu posed the following question: "Why do you think God created
us?" Responding to his own question, he said, "God created us not
because God is lonely and needs us but because God loves us and
wants us."

The Archbishop understood something about God that I needed
to grasp more fully. There is a massive difference between God needing us and God wanting us. We need to remind ourselves that God
already had a rich and fully sufficient friendship life in the Godhead
without humans around. Just imagine the giving and the loving and
the caring that was going on all the time among the Father, the Son,
and the Holy Spirit long before we came upon the scene. Out of the
abundance of this divine relational life—not out of any need of us—
God created our first ancestors. Put another way, God desired us
into existence because God passionately longs to be friends with us.

We are not on earth by accident or mistake or chance. There
are no illegitimate children in this world. We are here because God
wants us here. We have been desired into life. Our very existence
embodies God's passionate longing for our friendship. Perhaps our
aching for intimacy echoes the ache in God's heart as God grieves
our resistance to the Divine Friendship for which our hearts have
been shaped. Could it also be that our loneliness without a face

described in the first chapter is God's way of drawing us toward divine friendship?

The Bible tells us we are not meant to be alone. (See Genesis 2:18.) Because we have been made in the image of a relational God, we are divinely designed for relationship. We have been made by love, in love, to love. We are wired for friendship both human and divine. This is why we experience our most painful heartache and heartbreak in times of loneliness. But I offer good news: In that dark, lonely space, God comes looking for us, calling out for our friendship and partnership.

Where Are You?

The first question in the Bible draws us powerfully into God's passionate longing for friendship with us. We see it in the second creation story in Genesis 2:4–3:24. After creating Adam and Eve, God gives them everything they need for a flourishing life—air to breathe, food to eat, work to do, and someone to love. God only forbids one thing: They must not eat the fruit from the tree in the middle of the garden for then they will enter into rivalry with God.

We all know how the story unfolds from there. Adam and Eve refuse to take God's warning seriously. They eat the fruit that they have been told not to eat to tragic consequence. Their intimate connection with God and each other is broken. Closeness is replaced by distance, intimacy by distrust, and love by fear. Adam and Eve sew fig leaves together to hide their nakedness from each other, and they hide from God behind some bushes in the garden. Then we read those haunting words that take us right into the loving heart of God: "But the LORD God called . . . 'Where are you?'" (Gen. 3:9).

God could have asked different questions that would have revealed a very different picture of God. If God were an angry parent, God would have asked, "How could you have done this after all I have done for you?" But God does not. If God wanted Adam and Eve to feel really bad about their actions, God would have asked,

"Why did you do this when I gave so much to you?" But God does not. Instead of these guilt-producing, conscience-pricking questions, God simply asks, "Where are you?"

As we consider this question, does it help us realize how dearly God wants to be our friend? Certainly, God's question shows us that even when we mess up, when we let ourselves down, when we fail to obey God, God does not reject us. Nor does God give up on us. Rather God comes looking for us. God continues to pursue our companionship. God knows the worst about us, but that knowledge does not prevent God from taking the initiative in reaching out to us. Here's the bottom line of God's good news: Nothing can ever extinguish the flame of God's passionate longing to be our friend.

Recently I led a retreat for persons wanting to experience God more personally. During our first morning together, I encouraged them to imagine God asking them, "Where are you?" Then each participant wrote a letter from God expressing what God might say. This is what one man wrote down.

> Dear Bill, I miss you. I know that you feel ashamed about what you have done and have been trying to hide from me. I do not want you to feel any worse than you do. Instead, I want you to know that you are always on my mind. I would love to reconnect with you. I would love for us to be friends again. There are things that I want to say to you, and I would love to hear what is on your heart as well. Will you come out of hiding so that we can begin to live and work together again? Signed, Your Creator

friendship exercise

Take a few moments and try the same exercise. Read Genesis 3:8-10. Sit quietly with the following question: *Where are you?* Allow it to percolate in your heart and mind. What do you sense God saying to you through it? In the form of a personal letter addressed to you by God, write down in your own words what you think God may be saying to you. Ask yourself, *How do I feel about God inviting me into friendship? What steps can I take in response to this invitation?*

An Unexpected House Visit

In the Gospel of Luke, the writer introduces us to a diminutive tax collector named Zacchaeus. (See Luke 19:1-10.) We know that tax collectors in biblical times were despised. As a Jew who works for the Roman overlords, Zacchaeus is part of a corrupt system that causes many to see him as one of the chief sinners. He is not welcome in the local synagogue. Children spit in the dust when he passes by. Of all the people living in Jericho, he must be one of the loneliest.

When Jesus comes to Jericho, Zacchaeus desperately wants to see him. Why? Has he heard stories of how Jesus befriends those on the margins of society? We don't know. We do know that Zacchaeus is so eager to see Jesus that he climbs a tree to catch a better glimpse of him as he passes by. To Zacchaeus's absolute surprise and amazement, Jesus stops under the tree where he is perching, looks up, and says to him, "Zacchaeus, hurry and come down; for I must stay at your house today" (Luke 19:5).

We can imagine Zacchaeus's feelings—he feels accepted, recognized, and valued. Furthermore, because he knows Jesus is a prophet, there can be little doubt that he will interpret Jesus' request to visit his home as a sign that God accepts him and wants a relationship with him. No wonder Zacchaeus welcomes Jesus so warmly into his home. The dramatic encounter ends with Zacchaeus saying to Jesus that he will make immediate amends for all his past corrupt dealings. "Look, half of my possessions, Lord, I will give to the poor; and if I have defrauded anyone of anything, I will pay back four times as much" (Luke 19:8).

Talk about the power of God's transforming friendship! Change for Zacchaeus goes far beyond a change of heart; it involves facing the truth, making amends, and reconciling himself to others. His actions inevitably affect his relationships with those whom he has cheated, alter his own circumstances, and cause much conversation among those closest to him. By the time Zacchaeus has given half his possessions away and put things right with those whom he has wronged, he finds himself in a vastly different relational and economic life-space. Indeed, he has found a rare treasure. He has experienced the transformative effects of divine friendship.

One reason so many of us, both young and old, love this story is that we can identify strongly with Zacchaeus. Children, being small, often find themselves at the back of crowds and unable to see what is happening. Like Zacchaeus, we too may want to get closer to Jesus in our loneliness, but we think we are not good enough. So when Jesus takes the initiative and reaches out to Zacchaeus, his action demonstrates God's passionate longing to befriend us, no matter who we are or what we have done.

This story reminds us we don't have to have it all together before we can experience God's friendship. Jesus invites himself to Zacchaeus's house before the tax collector makes any significant lifestyle changes. Jesus doesn't say to him, "I will come to your house on the condition that you first get your life in order." Nor, it seems, does Jesus have to spell out to Zacchaeus what he needs to do. Zacchaeus's actions of radical repentance flow from the unconditional acceptance he receives from Jesus. Divine Friendship always sets us free to become the people God wants us to be, as it does with Zacchaeus.

friendship exercise

Read the story of Jesus and Zacchaeus in Luke 19:1-10. Ask the Holy Spirit to help you experience God's passionate longing for friendship with you. Use your imagination to picture the details of the scene—a busy street, crowds of people, Jesus passing by, Zacchaeus sitting in a nearby tree. You may even try to become part of the scene yourself. Watch the interactions among the people as you read the scripture. Listen to the conversations taking place. Observe the actions of each character. Finally, after five to ten minutes of praying this story imaginatively, pay attention to your own inner reactions and responses and talk about them with God.

An Image of Intimate Friendship

On the night before his execution, Jesus gave his disciples the simple yet profound illustration of the vine and the branches. (See John 15:1-8.) "I am the vine," he says to his followers; "you are the branches" (John 15:5). As his followers, they are to "abide" in him. The Greek word used here for "remain" is found numerous times in John's Gospel. Jesus not only wants them to serve as his disciples; he wants them to live with him in intimate friendship. This becomes even clearer when a few moments later he says to them, "I do not call you servants any longer . . . but I have called you friends, because I have made known to you everything that I heard from my Father" (John 15:15).

This image of the vine and branches reveals the remarkable depths of intimacy of the Divine Friendship into which we are invited. Jesus wants his followers to remain, dwell, live, and abide in him. At the beginning of the Gospel of John, two disciples ask Jesus, "Where are you staying?" (John 1:38). They want to make their home with Jesus. We too are invited to make our home in him and to let him make his home in us. When we respond to this invitation, as Jean Vanier describes, "We live a mutual indwelling. This indwelling is friendship."[2]

God desires to be as close to us as a vine to a branch. We have all experienced brief moments of intimate connection to God—perhaps as we walked along a beach, watched the sun set over the lake, sat alone in a coffee shop, sang a favorite hymn, or listened to a beautiful piece of music. But what Jesus offers us through this picture of the vine and the branches goes far beyond a fleeting awareness of being with God. Jesus invites us into a divine intimacy in which we daily live in him and he lives in us.

God deeply desires friendship with each one of us. To make that possible, God sends Jesus among us as the way into this friendship. As we come to abide in, remain in, and dwell in this Jesus who lives now as the risen Christ beyond crucifixion, he leads us into the intimate heart of God. The Gospel writers show us this daring offer, and the real-life experiences of Christ-followers throughout the ages have confirmed the truth that by abiding in Jesus we experience intimacy with God.

What does "abiding in Jesus" involve? It involves turning each day to Jesus, listening to his voice, sharing our hearts with him, nourishing ourselves on his words, following his commands, inviting him into everything we do, and joining him in giving life to others. It probably also entails pruning away those parts of our lives contaminated by selfishness and greed. As we walk with Jesus, he and his Father come to be with us and make their home with us. (See John 14:23.) We begin to live together in the intimacy of the divine friendship.

Before we move on, I want to make one more observation about abiding in Jesus. As we grow and mature and abide in Jesus, we will also find it necessary to remain in a community that celebrates him as Lord and friend. No vine has only one branch. We do not make the journey to God alone. There is no solitary Christ-follower. When we open our lives to Jesus, he comes with his arms around his brothers and sisters. As I've said before, our friendship with Jesus is *personal* but not *private*. To be connected to Jesus in friendship is to be connected to his friends as well. We will explore this more fully later when we look at God's dream for our world.

friendship exercise

Read John 15:1-8. Use your imagination in considering the image of the vine and the branches. Reflect on the intimate connection between a vine and its branches. It is difficult to know where one ends and the other begins. A simple and profound oneness exists

between them. The two combine almost as one in order to produce
ripe grapes. This is what it will be like between your Divine Friend
and you. When you give life to others by blessing them and by being
with them in a fully present way, it is neither you nor Jesus who
alone gives life. You and Jesus are working together. In the words
of Jean Vanier, "It is we and Jesus, Jesus in us and us in Jesus."[3] As
you reflect on this image, how does it help you imagine the intimate
nature of the Divine Friendship at work in your own life?

How has reading this chapter and engaging in the Friendship
Exercises affected you? My prayer is that you are coming to know
just how much God wants to be friends with you. Do not be discouraged if this has not happened. If you are still unsure about
whether God really wants your friendship, I encourage you to speak
about your misgivings with God and with someone you trust. Keep
reading. In the next chapter, you will explore how you can respond
to God's offer of Divine Friendship.

3

Getting to Know
Our Friend

Part of my ministry work that I find extremely challenging is conducting funerals. When I meet with the family members before the service, we always spend time talking about the person who has died. Then we plan the service. At this stage I will usually ask what hymns or songs they would like to sing. Even if they have no formal church connection, I am struck by how many times grieving family members ask for "What a Friend We Have in Jesus."

The choice is not surprising when we consider that the grief of losing a loved one is one of the hardest, loneliest, and most painful experiences we ever encounter. Singing of a faithful friend to whom we can bring everything in prayer, who will share our sorrows, and who knows our every weakness can bring immense comfort. Indeed, I want to suggest in this chapter that getting to know Jesus as our Divine Friend is the greatest treasure that life offers us. Through the centuries, millions of Christ-followers have testified with Paul the apostle that no heartache or heartbreak can ever separate us from the reality of God's love and intimate friendship made available to us in Jesus Christ. (See Romans 8:38-39.)

Friendship with Jesus, like our other friendships, begins and grows in ordinary ways. Building this friendship is not an other-worldly or mystical process but involves interacting with Jesus, getting to know God through him, meditating on the Gospel stories, taking Jesus' words seriously, and being open to the Holy Spirit.

The Bottom Line

By getting to know Jesus as our friend, we get to know God as God really is—that's the bottom line of the Christian faith. An exchange between the disciple Philip and Jesus clarifies this truth. Philip says to Jesus, "Lord, show us the Father, and we will be satisfied" (John 14:8). Jesus responds, "Have I been with you all this time, Philip, and you still do not know me? Whoever has seen me has seen the Father" (14:9).

The New Testament's open secret is this: As we keep company with Jesus, he leads us into the heart and life of God. What an astonishing bottom line this is! Certainly it has been for me. As I have grown older, I have come to recognize that God is always greater—greater than my theology, greater than my church tradition, greater than my experience. At times I wonder whether I can say anything about God without sounding trite or clichéd or arrogant. Truly, as the psalmist says, "Great is the LORD and most worthy of praise; his greatness no one can fathom" (Ps. 145:3, NIV). Jesus reveals this God to us—and what wonderful news that is! Because of Jesus' life with us, we can joyfully affirm truths about the boundless mystery of God.

In his book *Tokens of Trust: An Introduction to Christian Belief*, Rowan Williams provides a beautiful illustration to convey this amazing good news. He invites us to imagine ourselves attending a concert recital. We listen to a renowned pianist performing a great piece of music to the limit of her skill and concentration. All her strength, feeling, and love are focused on bringing to life the work and vision of the composer. In that moment, the passion of the composer comes through and saturates the performer's being during the time of the performance. In a nutshell, we meet the mind and the heart of the composer in the music played by the artist. In the same way, Jesus gives his whole life to perform the music God has composed. He performs the musical notes of God's passionate longing for a friendship with us throughout his life without a break, without a false note, without a stumble. Yet he remains his human self; all that makes him distinctively human shines through this creative work. While his life in our midst is fully human in every action, every word, every gesture, a divine love song can be perfectly heard. Jesus, through his words and life, his dying and rising, shows us what God is really like.[1]

Growing our friendship with Jesus is essential because through our relationship with him we encounter God as well. As we walk with Jesus, we find that God is always with us. As we listen to him, we hear God speaking to us. As we follow him, he leads us into God's river of life at its deepest. The kingdom of God is all around us right where we are, freely available and accessible to us through Jesus. The glorious invitation of the Christian message becomes clear—learn to live each day with simple confidence as one of Jesus' friends and he will, through his companionship, impart an eternal and indestructible kind of life to each one of us.

In order to enter into such a relationship, we must first decide to become a friend of Jesus. We don't just drift into friendship with him. Being his friend, like being anyone's friend, requires a definite, specific choice. We have to consciously decide to turn to him, to open our lives to his presence, and to entrust ourselves to him. However, this is only the beginning of the journey. To grow in friendship with Jesus takes time; friendship deepens gradually through many stages along the way. But it has to begin somewhere.

friendship exercise

Plan some time to be alone. Have paper and pen or pencil—or laptop or tablet—with you. During your alone time, write a letter to Jesus expressing your desire to enter into friendship with him. Describe what it is in Jesus that attracts you. If you feel doubtful or resistant, write about those feelings as well. Read your letter aloud to Jesus. Once you have done this, you may want to share your letter with someone you trust.

Meditating on Gospel Stories

In our significant friendships we become part of the inner lives of those persons. We get to know what they think and feel, what they value and dream, and more. The process of getting to know a friend in this way takes time, effort, and patience. It cannot be forced or sped up; there is no shortcut. Our love for the person and our desire to come to know this individual for who she or he really is keeps us going. Along the way we may discover qualities of our friend that we don't like. As a result, at times we may find ourselves resisting the demands and challenges of that friendship. We may even want to opt out of the relationship.

We may have a similar experience in our friendship with Jesus if it is to become a guiding light in our lives. Knowing Jesus personally differs from learning about him. Learning about Jesus involves acquiring historical information like where he was born, where he spent his life, and what he did in his ministry. Knowing Jesus personally means receiving the intimate knowledge that comes from living with Jesus each day and entering into his heart and mind, just as we do with our other friends. *Knowing* Jesus is more important than *knowing about* him.

But how can we know Jesus? The best way is to keep company with him by reading the Gospels meditatively. I first learned how to do this kind of reading over twenty years ago when I received

The Spiritual Exercises of Saint Ignatius of Loyola from an Anglican priest. The book encourages us to take a focused journey with Jesus through the Gospels. This journey can be accomplished either in a thirty-day residential retreat setting or over a period of about nine months in daily life. A large part of the journey is devoted to getting to know Jesus personally through Gospel contemplations. I will describe how to pray with the Gospels in this way.

friendship exercise

Set aside about twenty minutes. Begin your time by asking Jesus for help. After all, if you want to grow your friendship with Jesus, he has to reveal himself to you. He has to show you his heart and mind so that you can come to know him. Ask in prayer, *Lord, reveal yourself to me that I may come to know you better, love you more deeply, and follow you more closely.* Then, take a Gospel story, read it slowly a few times, and allow the story to freely awaken your imagination. Some people have a vivid way of imagining; they "see" the details of the Gospel story clearly. Others, like myself, "sense" the details in a more intuitive way. You can imagine with all your senses, not just sight.

As you allow your imagination to interact with Jesus in the story, Christ's risen presence accompanies you. You can trust that he will encourage you in your friendship by showing himself to you in some way. Perhaps he will show you some aspect of his own relationship with the Father or his compassion for people in pain or his anger against injustice. Whatever he reveals, you can bet that it will stir up reactions in you that you can share with him in conversation. As you faithfully keep company with Jesus in this way, you slowly get to know him personally, and your friendship matures and deepens.

Take time now to meditate on a Gospel story on your own. Like swimming or riding a bicycle, you learn by doing and not by reading. Remember to begin your time by asking the Lord to reveal himself to you. You may need to return to this request a few times during your time of prayer. Don't forget to pay attention to your own thoughts and feelings, whatever they are, and share them with the Lord. If you don't have a Gospel story in mind, I suggest the following options: Jesus' baptism (Matthew 3:13-17), Jesus' healing of a paralyzed man (John 5:1-8), or Jesus' washing of his disciples' feet (John 13:1-17). Meditating on the Gospels creates a solid foundation for your friendship with Jesus, allows you to get to know him more personally, and draws you into a practical obedience to him.

Doing What Jesus Said

Once we have begun a friendship with Jesus, we will want to please him in everything we do. As he says, "You are my friends if you do what I command you" (John 15:14). Thankfully, as we seek to do this, Jesus comes alongside us to offer help. We would struggle to obey him otherwise. With all our inner struggles and bad habits, obeying Jesus' commands can be difficult. But with him as our friend, we are able to see and do what is good. This is why Jesus tells his disciples, "Anyone who loves me will obey my teaching. My Father will love them, and we will come to them and make our home with them" (John 14:23, NIV).

Jesus does not impose his teachings on us in a heavy or burdensome way. He is not out to spoil our lives. If we are feeling overwhelmed, we can remember that he is our Friend who loves us and wants the best for us. He wants us to experience abundant life—life at its very best. He longs for us to become the people we are meant to be. He wants God's wounded world to be made whole. For these reasons, Jesus tells us to put his words into practice. It is for our ultimate good. This is why Peter says to him, "Lord, to whom can we go? You have the words of eternal life" (John 6:68).

As we endeavor to deepen our relationship with Jesus, I believe we should pay special attention to his teachings. When we read his words in the Gospels, it will not be long before we notice the absolute centrality of love in his overall teaching—"You shall love the

Lord your God with all your heart, and with all your soul, and with all your mind.' . . . And a second is like it: 'You shall love your neighbor as yourself'" (Matt. 22:37, 39). Everything else Jesus teaches flows from this central teaching into the various situations in which we find ourselves. For example, teachings like "bless those who curse you" (Luke 6:28), "do not judge" (Matt. 7:1), and "love your enemies" (Matt. 5:44) translate the words of the Great Commandment into specific life circumstances so that we don't misunderstand what love demands or become sentimental about what Jesus meant by love.

We can begin the journey of practical obedience by making a conscious decision to become loving persons. We will need all the help we can get. My greatest failures are failures in loving, especially with those closest to me. One recent example comes immediately to mind. The other day I shared with my spiritual director the sudden reemergence of a destructive pattern in my marriage. For a few weeks Debbie had been going through a challenging time in her work as a teacher. From before sunrise until near midnight, she would be engrossed in lesson preparation, report writing, and grading papers. By her own admission she had little energy left over to invest in our relationship, but she looked forward to doing so when the difficult time was over.

Instead of moving toward Debbie during this unusually pressure-filled time, I became politely distant, even though I knew it would hurt her. When she asked how I was, I shrugged off her concern, blocking her attempts to show me her care. I had struggled a great deal with this tendency in the earlier years of our marriage, often withdrawing for days from Debbie into a cold and sullen silence. Thankfully, with the help of God and the wise counsel of some insightful companions, I had made some progress in getting to the root of the problem and overcoming this behavioral pattern. Yet this pattern was reappearing, causing pain to the one I loved and leaving me discouraged both as a husband and as a Christ-follower.

After I finished describing what was happening in my marriage, my spiritual director asked this intriguing question: "How have you experienced God's love during this time?" I thought for a while and then mentioned a few ways in which God's love had come to me in those weeks. During that time God had opened up some wonderful opportunities for ministry. The outcomes of these ministry efforts had far exceeded my human abilities, giving clear evidence of God's support and involvement. Above all, in spite of my failures to love Debbie well, God had remained lovingly present in my life as my Divine Friend through it all. My companion listened as I listed these examples and then extended an invitation. Would I be willing to spend some time talking with God about how I could love Debbie in her difficult time as God had loved me?

I started this conversation with God immediately on the drive home. In the silence of the car, I had the sense of God encouraging me: *When you get back home, confess to Debbie how you have been treating her. Receive my forgiveness and let me continue to heal your heart. Do not ever give up on learning to love. Start loving her the way I have loved you. Open up opportunities for her to love you. Help her in whatever way you can to get through this difficult time. Rather than withdrawing, offer her your wholehearted presence and attention. As you give yourself in these ways, know that I will be with you and will help you.*

I am learning through all my failures in loving that obeying Jesus requires more than simply trying harder to change my behavior. Obviously we do the best we can to love others better. We learn how to listen more carefully. We develop skills to communicate more effectively. We practice conflict-resolution strategies. All these efforts help, but what we most need is to become loving people from the inside out. We need the transforming friendship of Jesus as a constant reality. He alone, through his companionship with us, can reproduce his kind of love in us.

friendship exercise

Think of someone who struggles with the loneliness of grief. Give some thought, attention, and prayer to how you might express love to this person. If my experience is anything to go by, you will feel totally inadequate. You can never take away a grieving person's lone-liness. So what can you do? In your inadequacy you can ask your Divine Friend to be with you and to befriend your grieving neighbor through your presence and care.

When you are with the person, refrain from trying to "fix" his or her grief. You cannot tell someone how to feel or what to think or what to do. Stay away from any God language that may sound hol-low, superficial, or empty. Instead, offer the gift of your listening presence, your thoughtful attention, and your loving care. Ask the Lord to touch his or her life through your friendship.

Some time ago I read *Never Alone: A Personal Way to God* by Joseph F. Girzone. The author dedicated his book to Jesus. I found that ges-ture very moving, so I thought I would try to do something similar with this chapter.

> I dedicate this chapter to my Divine Friend who stays with me always in my heart. As a young person, he met me where I was, accepted me as I was, and drew me into the life that I now live. Through his words he continues to show me how to build my life upon a rock rather than on sand. Even though I fail to love in the way he wants me to, he never gives up on me. In those times when I struggle with loneliness, doubt, and anxiety, he does not leave me to face life on my own. Rather he often shows me the next step to take. Sometimes I experience a wild joy that I know can only have come from him. He can be your friend too if you want him to. Do not be afraid. He wants you to become freer and more joyful than you have ever been before. He longs for you to become his friend. If you do, I can promise that you will never be alone.[2]

4

Understanding Prayer as Deepening Friendship

O nce I started living in the divine friendship, I began the process of learning how to pray. I must confess I still feel like a beginner. It does not surprise me one bit that the only time the disciples ask Jesus to teach them anything, they say, "Lord, teach us to pray" (Luke 11:1). Even though they have been raised within the Jewish faith and worship in the local synagogue, they still want to know how to pray. I can identify with them.

Just before South Africa became a democracy, the church of which I am part engaged in a process called "Journey to a New Land." As a church we wanted to establish our mission priorities in a postapartheid era. As part of this process, church members received a questionnaire asking what they were looking for from their church. Over twenty-five thousand members responded, and the most frequent request was for a living spirituality. Strikingly, those who made this request were already involved in worshiping and praying within their local congregations.

Behind this request I believe there exists a profound longing: We want to experience God in a conscious, personal, and intimate way. There are things we want to know. Are we orphans alone in this vast, expanding universe? Is there someone who knows that we are here, who is interested in our little lives, and who has our best interests at heart? Is there another reality besides the material? Theological debates and conversations only take us so far. We have to come to know for ourselves the reality of the living God. This personal sense of knowing comes primarily through our experience of prayer.

We have explored two basic convictions concerning God's transformation of our loneliness. First, within God's heart resides a passionate longing for friendship with us. Second, our response to this good news takes the shape of becoming a friend of Jesus. Prayer can deepen that friendship. Whatever makes for good friendship makes for good prayer. M. Basil Pennington puts it well when he writes, "Prayer is friendship in action—that high point of friendship when we are simply entering into and experiencing the reality that we and God are friends."[1]

friendship exercise

Think of one significant friendship you currently enjoy. How did this friendship begin and grow? What activities nourish this friendship? What do you value most about your friend? How do you contribute to the friendship? Make a list of your responses. Identify any clues that could help you deepen your life of prayer with your Divine Friend.

Intentionality

Good friendships take time, effort, and planning. A couple of times each month Debbie and I meet with our friends—another married couple—either at one of our homes or at a restaurant. This simple arrangement requires one or two phone calls, deciding on a time and place, and all of us actually showing up. Sometimes we carry on when we don't feel like it. The other day I got the following text message from the husband: "Thank you for our many Friday nights together. Even though there have been those rare moments when I have not felt like going out, I have always felt better after our time together."

We need a similar intentionality in our life of prayer. Often people will tell me that they don't need to pray at specific times because they speak with God all the time. I have little doubt that God is always with us, but the quality of our ongoing conversation depends mostly on whether we set aside time on a regular basis to be together. We will pray *always* if we pray intentionally *sometimes*. If we want to deepen our prayer lives, we must create a space to be with God.

This divine appointment can happen in a variety of ways. Some people carve out small amounts of time each day. Others prefer to block out longer periods of time once or twice a week. The challenge comes in discovering the best possible times for prayer. What works for a young mother with two small kids will differ from what works for a retired person. We should be realistic in shaping the rhythm of prayer to the rhythm of our lives. The key factor is intentionality in planning this time.

Often we have to rethink the way we presently use our time. Most of us find the time to do what we deem important. We give time to eating, to sleeping, to our daily work, to our favorite TV programs, and so on. If our friendship with God is as significant as we say it is, then our schedule needs to reflect this value. Reordering priorities creates challenges. If we are not producing or doing something worthwhile or ticking off a task from our to-do list, we feel we are wasting our time. But prayer—though not a waste of time—can feel like we are "doing nothing." On the contrary, prayer involves an intentional commitment to pausing and spending time with our

Divine Friend. A transforming friendship with God simply does not occur without prayer.

Closely related to planning specific times to be with God is finding a suitable place to pray. We need to be thoughtful, wise, and creative about this choice. Where will we not be interrupted? Is there a place that is not too noisy? Would this place be where we live or somewhere else like a nearby church? We read in the Gospels that in order to spend uninterrupted time with his Father, Jesus will often go to a "lonely place" for prayer. Little wonder that when he gives instructions about praying, he emphasizes the importance of such a place: "When you pray, go into your room, close the door and pray to your Father, who is unseen" (Matt. 6:6, NIV).

friendship exercise

Reflect on the past week. How have you spent your time? What are your thoughts and feelings about the way you spend your time? Does your appointment calendar reflect what you say is important to you? What is God saying to you through your life at the moment? In light of this reflection, decide when you will spend one-on-one time with God. Write it down in your agenda or put it into your digital calendar so that nothing else will intrude on that time.

Now think about a place where you can be alone with your Divine Friend—a special chair in the family room, a corner in a bedroom, or, if you are fortunate, a spare room that you can convert into a prayer space. Sometimes you can set apart a space for prayer with a symbol—a candle, an icon, a crucifix, or a cross. You may decide to make your prayer place away from home—going to your car at lunchtime, stopping at an open church, or setting aside a chair at your place of work. Again, intentionality is critical in choosing a place for prayer. Consistency and routine help sustain the habit.

Conversation

Friendships flourish when people engage in healthy conversation. When we get together with a friend, we spend our time talking with and listening to each other. We share what is happening in our lives, and our friend shares as well. We do our best to be attentive to what is being shared. Both parts of conversation—sharing and listening—make for an enjoyable time together. If one individual is unwilling to share or constantly interrupts or hogs the conversation, the time may be spoiled. Each person needs to speak and to listen for good communication to take place.

Our friendship with God grows as we talk with the risen Christ. (As we noted earlier, abiding in Jesus and growing in intimate friendship with God are connected.) I remember how I first spoke with Jesus as a young person. Every night before I went to sleep I would put an empty chair next to my bed. Then I imagined Jesus sitting in the chair. I would share with him aloud what was happening in my life. My conversation with him included how I was feeling at that moment, what I was grateful for, what I was sorry about, what concerned me, and what I needed help facing. I continued this method of prayer for a number of years until I began learning to listen as well.

I continue to talk aloud to my Divine Friend. Just recently I spent a few days alone. One afternoon I decided to use an empty chair again in my praying. As I sat across from where I imagined Jesus to be sitting, my mind went back to those early days when I had just begun to pray. For about an hour I reflected on what my friendship with Jesus had meant to me since my sixteenth year and spoke my thoughts and feelings aloud with him. Tears of overwhelming gratitude and thankfulness ambushed me.

We never outgrow the need to speak personally and directly with our Divine Friend. Teresa of Avila, a great teacher on prayer from the sixteenth century, insisted on the need to constantly share ourselves with God. She also named one crucial condition: We must think about what we are saying. Talking to God without thinking about what we are actually saying insults God and puts our praying into the category of superstition and magic. However, Teresa believed that thoughtful spoken prayer could take us into the very depths of communion with God.

Additionally, like in any good friendship, we need to listen to God. This part of our conversation with God usually takes much longer to develop. We may find listening carefully to someone we can see to be difficult—but what about someone we cannot see? The act of listening to someone we cannot see may raise questions. What does it mean to say that God talks to us? How does this happen? How do we know we are not just talking to ourselves? And since we feel unsure about these matters, we often end up talking all the time. Prayer then becomes a one-way "conversation," which is not good for any friendship.

All these questions have been part of my own prayer journey. Thankfully, over the years some wonderful mentors and teachers have guided me. I can summarize what I've learned about listening to God in one particular insight: However God chooses to speak to us—through a sudden memory, a strong feeling, a flash of insight, the words of a friend, the mysteries of creation, or, most often, the Bible—God's voice in our experience usually takes the shape of a certain kind of thought.[2]

I have been learning not to do all the talking during my prayer time. In the same way that I can only listen to others if I keep quiet, I must stop talking to God if I am going to pay attention to what God is saying to me. In my one-on-one time with God, there are moments when I am silent. During these moments I think about what I have read in scripture, I contemplate a Gospel story, I reflect on my time of conversation with Christ, or I recall the events of the day. During these times, I pay attention to my thoughts and feelings and wonder what God may be saying to me.

But how do we know if what we perceive is from God? What criteria can we rely on for discerning that a thought comes from God and not from some other source? Thoughts from God have a distinctive feel, content, and texture about them. They have those characteristics outlined in James 3:17: "The wisdom that comes from heaven is first of all pure; then peace-loving, considerate, submissive, full of mercy and good fruit, impartial and sincere" (NIV). Above all, whatever God says to us will always be consistent with the teachings of Jesus that we find in the Gospels. This is why an intimate acquaintance with his words is so critical.

Sometimes when we need to know what God is saying about a particular situation but no thoughts distinctly stand out, it can be useful to imagine what God might be saying. We do this in our ordinary friendships. On the basis of our times spent together, we have a hunch what a good friend will say to us. For example, if I were to consider what my friends think about the present South African situation, what values are significant for business, or what they feel about our relationship, I could predict with some accuracy what they would say. Through our shared times together I have come to know their minds on certain matters. It can work that way with God too.

friendship exercise

Speak with God about one situation in your life at the moment. Then stop talking, sit in silence, and ask yourself, *In the light of what I have come to know about God in the Bible through the teachings of Jesus in the Gospels, through what I have learned in my faith community, and through my own experience of the divine friendship over the years, what do I think God might be saying to me about this situation?* Consider your response, perhaps writing it down for further reflection, and speak about it with someone you trust.

Transparency

Good friendships invite, nurture, and require growing transparency. One of the most valuable aspects of the friendship Debbie and I enjoy with another couple is the growing freedom we have to be honest with one another. As trust has developed among us, we have removed the masks we sometimes wear. This trust has not appeared overnight. When any of us have harbored feelings of disappointment or resentment and not expressed them, our friendship has limped along politely. But as we have gradually taken the risk of self-disclosure and vulnerability, the friendship bonds among us have strengthened and become a source of much joy.

The parallels between our human relationships and our divine friendship stand out strongly. When we do not express what we are thinking and feeling to God, a sense of distance grows between us. Telltale symptoms indicate that we are not being emotionally honest with God: boredom, staleness, and dull formality in our prayer lives. Whenever we keep our more negative feelings and attitudes away from God in prayer, we hinder the formation of intimacy. I have heard it said that Martin Luther once suggested the following as the most meaningful principle for growing a life of prayer: Don't lie to God!

What does this transparency look like in practice? It means sharing what we actually think and feel as opposed to what we believe we should say. Polite prayer poisons our relationship with God. Honest prayer involves stating our doubts and disappointments, our anger and resentment, our loneliness and grief. Sometimes we may verbalize powerful feelings of anger, bitterness, and even hatred toward God. James Martin, SJ, well-known writer on Ignatian spirituality, sums it up for me when he says, "Be honest with God about everything."[3]

Some people see this practice as a waste of time because God knows what we want to say anyway. I don't agree. The purpose of being transparent with God is not to give information to God. The purpose is to develop intimacy with God. A moment with my daughter illustrates the effect of transparency. Some months ago she faced a lengthy operation on her jaw. I knew of her apprehension about what could go wrong. On the Sunday before the surgery, she came to church to hear me preach. After the service she approached and said, "I am scared about the operation. Will you pray with me?" In that moment she was not giving me information that I did not already have. She was sharing vulnerably and, by being totally honest, deepening the closeness of our relationship.

friendship exercise

Find some time to be alone with your Divine Friend. Share with God whatever you are feeling right now about your relationship. You may be feeling gratitude, regret, disappointment, anger, longing, or a sense of being forsaken. Whatever your feelings may be, find words to express yourself aloud to God as honestly as you can.

In this chapter we have looked at prayer as the means of deepening friendship. Obviously the practice of prayer involves more than what I have written here. But other types of prayer—such as intercessory prayer, ministering to others in healing prayer, deliverance prayer—only find their proper place when we are in healthy relationship with God ourselves. And if we really want to be good friends with God and experience that intimate connection for which we have been made, we will need to share in conversation with God in an intentional and transparent way.

5

Looking Outward Together

I recently spent time with a young couple who were obviously very much in love. They held hands, constantly checked with each other about what they were saying, and gazed into each other's eyes. They clearly meant the world to each other. They spoke about how they met, their feelings about their relationship, and their dreams for the future. The youthful freshness of their love was tangible. As I glimpsed their newfound delight and joy, I felt happy for them.

Reflecting later, I thought about how intimate relationships develop. When we fall in love, we normally only have eyes for our partner. We want to spend lots of time together, to get to know the other person as much as possible, and to feel as close as we can. With time, however, healthy relationships move into another dimension. Gradually we open our relationship to those around us. We want to embrace others by enriching their lives and blessing them. We discover that mature intimacy encompasses not just looking into each other's eyes but also looking outward together in the same direction.

A similar evolution happens in our relationship with Jesus. In the early stages, we may have eyes only for him. We might call this the "courtship phase." But as our friendship grows, he gradually turns our eyes to look in the same direction he is looking. No longer is the divine friendship a cozy, private one. We start to look outward together through his eyes. I want to explore what this shift in focus means. If we neglect this dimension, we can be sure that our friendship with Jesus will remain adolescent. We will not grow up to become adult children of God, sharing a mature intimacy with the Creator.

God's Dream

In order to look outward in the same direction that the risen Christ looks, we need to examine the direction in which he looked when he was on earth. From the beginning of his public ministry, Jesus' life and message revolve totally around God's dream for the world. In language familiar to first-century Jews, Jesus calls this dream, "the kingdom of God." God's kingdom is where God rules and reigns, where God's will is done, and where what God wants to happen really does happen. Wherever Jesus goes, he makes that dream a reality. He lives out God's dream and calls every man and woman and child to join him.

As staggering as it sounds, I assert that friendship lies at the heart of God's dream. We explored God's passionate longing for our friendship in the second chapter. The Creator whom we meet in Jesus Christ deeply longs to be friends with us. William A. Barry, SJ, expands this thought a little more when he writes, "God wants a world where we human beings live in harmony and friendship with God, with one another, and with the rest of creation, cooperating with God wherever we are."[1] For this central vision Jesus came and lived and gave his life for us.

How does Jesus live out God's dream? First, through his words. He constantly tells those around him that they are important to

God. On one occasion he draws a comparison between people and birds: "Are not five sparrows sold for two pennies? Yet not one of them is forgotten in God's sight. But even the hairs of your head are all counted. Do not be afraid; you are of more value than many sparrows" (Luke 12:6-7). What a powerful effect those words would have on the lives of those who listened to him! Without a shadow of doubt they would know that Jesus and his Father of whom he always spoke care about them and want to be friends with them.

Second, Jesus lives out God's dream through his actions. He acts as though every individual holds infinite value. Whether he is blessing a little child, touching an outcast leper living on the margins of society, visiting the home of a despised tax collector, or responding to the cry of a blind beggar on the roadside, Jesus treats everyone he meets with immeasurable respect and care. His actions show others that in spite of what they have done or are going through, God loves them and wants to be their friend. Imagine their joy and delight in knowing that the Creator of the universe longs for their personal friendship and company!

Third, and most crucial, is Jesus' sacrificial death. Jesus most visibly demonstrates God's dream for friendship with us on the cross. A few hours before his execution, Jesus says to his closest friends, "No one has greater love than this, to lay down one's life for one's friends" (John 15:13). Through his death he wants to show us nothing will ever stop him—and the God whom he serves—from wanting to be friends with us, not even our sin. In fact, the apostle Paul later confidently writes, "But God proves his love for us in that while we still were sinners Christ died for us" (Rom. 5:8).

As friends of Jesus, each of us is called to make God's dream our own. By doing so, we begin to look outward with Jesus. God invites us to work toward making God's dream a reality wherever we find ourselves. In creating this world, God did not dream of lonely neighbors and broken relationships, unchecked greed and desperate poverty, violent crime and environmental pollution, corruption and hatred. God calls us to live in tune with God's dream within these nightmarish realities. But how and where do we start? I suggest that we begin to look outward in three ways. But first, a friendship exercise.

friendship exercise

If God truly dreams of a world where you live as a friend to God and in harmony with others and the rest of creation, what does this look like in practical terms? What would God's dream look like in your home, at your place of work, in your community? What are the major obstacles to turning your home, place of work, or community into God's dream? Write down some of the thoughts and pictures that come to your mind as you think about what God's dream would look like in your immediate world.

Our Closest Neighbors

Jesus expresses God's dream by making friends with those around him. He consistently reaches out to people with compassion, acceptance, and forgiveness. Even when Judas betrays him, Jesus addresses him with the word *friend*. (See Matthew 26:50.) His example reminds us that we live in tune with God's dream by learning to live in friendship with those around us. God desires people living in harmony with God and with one another. By reaching out in friendship, we make God's dream a reality in our surroundings.

We can begin wherever we are—with our families, with the people next door, with colleagues at work, with the people who serve us in supermarkets and banks, or even with those who seem radically different from us. Every human encounter can become a sacred conversation. Each day we can look outward toward our closest neighbors and ask God to help us become a little less self-centered and a little more other-centered. The most important place for us to make God's dream a reality is always in our interactions with our closest neighbors.

However, I offer a word of caution. We are called to befriend others without the desire to try to change them. How would we feel if we knew someone only wanted to be our friend because he or she had an agenda for our lives? To me, that feels more like a consumer relationship in which I am a target market rather than a genuine friendship in which I feel valued as an individual. When we enter into friendships with others, we must remind ourselves that the Holy Spirit changes people. In contrast, building agenda-less friendships enables God to make God's dream a reality in our daily encounters.

A few months ago, I officiated the memorial service for the mother of a close friend. Her name was Sulette Smith. As I got to know her through the reflections of those closest to her, I learned she was someone who lived in tune with God's dream for this world. Sulette generously and warmly befriended those around her. Her son, Tom, offered the following words about his mother:

> My mother was an introvert who lived in deep friendships with the people and the animals around her. Her life was like the solid jacaranda tree in front of her house, casting a loving shadow. With her behind-the-scenes life, Mom created loving spaces for other people. When she passed away, news of her death spread. The people who were touched by her ordinary, everyday interactions testified to her loving life. The hairdresser, launderer, garden service coordinator, and nurses all testified to Mom's ability to be a friend. . . . Through listening to other people she became an ear-oasis for many. Her listening life was a sacrament of God's friendship with us. Many of my friends told me how they experienced her steadfast love for Jesus and her welcoming gentleness. As I read through her journals, I found the footprints of a deep, daily friendship with Jesus. This friendship scented her friendships with people, animals, and the whole created order.

friendship exercise

List two or three people outside your immediate family circle with whom you interact on a regular basis. Give some prayer, thought, and attention to how you can express genuine friendship to these individuals. Usually one of the best ways to do this is simply to take a genuine interest in their lives. As you get to know them, express your care for them in whatever way seems appropriate. Ask the Holy Spirit to make God's dream for their lives more real through your friendship.

Our Daily Work

For most of us, the main purpose of work is to provide for ourselves and for those who depend on us. I like the story of the businessman who, while jogging early one morning, found his pathway blocked by a worker digging a ditch.

"What are you doing?" inquired the jogger, rather put out by the inconvenience of having to find an alternate route.

"I'm digging a ditch," replied the worker, wiping the sweat from his face.

"Why?" asked the irate jogger.

"Well," said the worker, "I'm digging this ditch . . . to get the money . . . to buy the food . . . to get the strength . . . to dig this ditch."

As friends of Jesus, we need to look at our daily work from a new perspective. While our daily work provides a living for our families and for ourselves, there is more to it. Our work also provides a significant arena for living in tune with God's dream. When we enter into the divine friendship, we don't have to become monks or nuns or ordained ministers in order to work with God. Rather, we can recognize our daily work as the primary opportunity to partner with God in making God's dream for this world a reality. I often say to my congregation that the most important mission trip we make is the daily journey to our places of work.

What does it mean to see our places of employment as a chance to partner with God? Here are some basic thoughts. Work is the place where we learn how to love God and serve our neighbor. It is where we help to provide for the needs—technical, commercial, mechanical, intellectual, and so on—of people in our community so that we can live together in harmony. It is indeed the primary place where we are learning how to do our daily work in cooperation with God and in the power of God. So while it is the place where we provide for ourselves and for our loved ones, it is also where we live out and extend God's dream for a world in which people can live in *shalom*—or well-being in the widest sense of the word.

When we don't envision our work as a way to fulfill God's dream, we drive a wedge between our daily lives and our journeys of faith. We develop a split-spirituality between those "spiritual" parts of our lives where we live with God and those "secular" parts where we live as though we are on our own. Moreover, we stop God's dream from becoming a greater reality in the place where we spend most of our waking hours. We each possess a unique way of extending God's kingdom to our workplaces, and God depends on our cooperation in this adventure.

I have a friend who takes Jesus' invitation to make God's dream real in the workplace very seriously. For many years he lived out his Christian call at a crane company; now he works as a trainer in different corporate settings. I remember a conversation with him after his pastor asked him to attend another meeting at his local church. His reply reminds us of our calling to live in tune with God's dream where life places us throughout our workday.

> I don't want to spend any more time doing church things. Each day, Monday through Friday, I am at work. I leave home at seven in the morning, and I get home at six. That's where I need to be a Christ-follower—at work—not just on church property. I need help with some of the ethical issues I am dealing with in the workplace. I need to know what it means to genuinely love and serve others at work. I need to know how to ensure that my work will promote goodness and

blessings in my surroundings. When I get home from work, I don't want to go out again to do ministry at church. I have been trying to live as Jesus' friend all day at my job.

friendship exercise

Each day this week as you do your mission trip to work, accept the invitation to make God's dream a reality. Throughout the day, ask God to accompany you in each activity. One of the best descriptions of prayer I know of is the following: "Talking to God about what we are doing together."[2] Make a note of the effects of this approach as you go through your day. Observe what happens in your relationships, in how you do your work, and in the outcomes of your efforts. Bringing prayer and daily work together will carry you through the day with an awareness of God's presence with and around you.

Our Broken Community

Obviously we cannot befriend all those living in need and misery around us. We cannot connect with all the sick and bereaved and dying. We cannot minister to all the poor, empower all the economically disadvantaged, educate all those who are illiterate, visit all those in prison. But in our conversations with our Divine Friend, we can ask, "What is my little piece of God's dream? Whom can I serve?" These kinds of questions, when accompanied by persistent prayer and followed-up with purposeful action, begin to make God's dream a reality.

Over the years I have been struck by the connection between our little piece of God's dream and our own pain. Often the seeds of a personal calling lie buried in our own suffering. As we pay attention to our own pain, we sometimes sense God beckoning us to reach out to others who struggle in similar ways. Is God asking us to use our suffering to bring healing and blessing to those around us? I have seen this happen repeatedly in the lives of those whom I pastor, and I will share some of their stories.

Ivan and Norma had three children, two of whom were born with severe disabilities. I shared many conversations with them as they sought to work through their anguish and despair. Through their pain they were led to initiate a ministry to other parents in similar situations. Their pioneering efforts resulted in the birth of a small community of friends made up of parents, their children, and helpers who wanted to be part of the ministry. For over eight years they gathered every month to celebrate their faith, share their stories and struggles, and play together.

A few years ago one of Mark and Belinda's children died tragically. Few days went by without the pangs of unimaginable pain and loss. Their grief hugely impacted their marriage, how they viewed their lives, and the way they understood their faith. After spending months processing their thoughts and feelings of grief, Belinda decided that she would like to work with other parents whose children had died. She got involved in the work of Compassionate Friends, and she became one of their key resource persons in the counseling of other grieving parents.

John battled alcoholism for years. One night in desperation he got down on his knees and called out to God for help. With the support of the 12-step program of Alcoholics Anonymous (AA), he discovered a life of sobriety, sanity, and serenity. Today, after thirty years without drinking, he continues to befriend others who battle alcohol addiction. Besides regularly attending his local AA meeting one night a week, John visits a rehabilitation facility to connect with those still imprisoned in the chains of addiction. Whenever he speaks publicly, he offers this message of hope to those battling addiction: "It doesn't have to be this way."

Jesus always invites us to look outward in the same direction he looks. In this way, we become aware of the human struggles around us in addition to becoming aware of our own pain. Jesus opens our eyes to see with fresh clarity both the beauty and the horror of our surroundings. When we look around our communities with our new eyesight, one particular human's suffering may penetrate our hearts more deeply than others. In that circumstance, God calls us personally to cooperate in making God's dream more real in our world.

friendship exercise

Spend some time quietly reflecting with God on the following questions. Make notes if it helps you to think more carefully.

- What have been some of your personal experiences of pain?
- How do they connect with the experiences of those around you?
- What human suffering in your community touches you the most?
- What are your special gifts? How could you use them to make God's dream become a reality in your local community?

As you reflect on your responses with your Divine Friend, be aware of clues about what your little piece of God's dream might be.

Let me restate the main point of this chapter: As friends of Jesus, we are invited to look outward with him in the same direction. His dream for the world is the same as God's dream. He calls us to live with him in tune with this dream. We do this through our friendships, our places of daily work, and our broken communities. A simple prayer can keep this invitation alive: *Lord Jesus, help me to make God's dream for the world a reality.*

6

Exploring Our Friend's Address Book

A few years ago I visited Tampa, Florida, for the first time. I had been asked to preach at Hyde Park United Methodist Church, and I arrived just as a hurricane headed toward the coastline. A couple from the church met me at the airport, settled me in my hotel room, and then took me out to supper. We had a wonderful evening getting to know one another over delicious Cuban cuisine. Around 10:00 p.m., we drove back to the hotel in pouring rain with almost no visibility. My adventure was only beginning.

After the couple dropped me off, I went up to my third-floor room. When I put my security key-card into its lock, the door would not open. Then I heard the sounds of human activity coming from inside my room. Thinking I was being robbed, I tried even harder to open the door. Still it would not open. Suddenly I wondered if perhaps this were not my room, and I feared the people inside thought that I was trying to rob them. What if they called hotel security to have me arrested?

I returned to the elevator, went down to reception, introduced myself to the receptionist, and asked for my room number. He logged into his computer, checked his records, and said to me, "Sir, we don't have you booked at this hotel." I wasn't sure what to do. Then it dawned on me that in the poor visibility my hosts had dropped me off at the wrong address. I discovered that this hotel was a member of the same franchise but on a different street from the hotel with my reservation. I needed to get the right address to find my hotel.

We always need to be sure we have the right address! During his time here on earth, Jesus prepares his friends for life without his physical presence by telling them about some addresses where he will continue to meet them. These instructions are scattered throughout the four Gospels. Gathered together I call them "Jesus' Address Book." In effect, Jesus says to the disciples and to us, "Explore these addresses. Here's where you will find my risen and ascended presence. If you spend time in these places and with these people, our friendship together will be nourished, and you will make God's dream a greater reality."

Now we know from scripture that the unpredictable God can surprise us in all things, in all places, and in all situations. God is always right where we are, wherever we are, here and now. Christ, we know, is found not only in one place but wherever we find ourselves. His risen and ascended presence, as the writer to the Ephesians puts it, fills the entire universe. (See Ephesians 4:10.) But there are some special Gospel addresses where our Divine Friend promises to meet us. I want to explore three of those addresses.

The First Gospel Address—Bread and Wine

On the night before he dies, Jesus eats with his closest friends. Gospel writer Mark describes the evening. "While they were eating, [Jesus] took a loaf of bread, and after blessing it he broke it, gave it to them, and said, 'Take; this is my body.' Then he took a cup, and after giving thanks he gave it to them, and all of them drank from it" (Mark 14:22-23). Our Divine Friend can be found whenever and wherever friends gather together to share in Communion. Indeed, in Holy Communion, Jesus Christ tells us he wants our friendship.

We celebrate many things when we eat the bread and drink the cup. We celebrate what God has done in Jesus, for it is his death and resurrection that give meaning to the elements. We celebrate God's dream for our world when all will share in friendship with God and one another. We celebrate how the ordinary things of life—bread and wine—point beyond themselves to the presence of God in all things. Above all, we celebrate that Christ is alive and present with us, coming to us in the moment we receive the bread and wine.

For centuries, followers of Jesus have debated and argued about what actually happens in Communion. Does the bread and wine literally become his body and blood? Or are they symbols? Are they signs? What are we doing when we eat the bread and drink the wine? These are critical questions. What we believe about them can affect how we celebrate the sacrament. But we can also miss Jesus in the midst of these heated discussions if we are not careful. Whatever else we might believe about Communion, the essential encounter is meeting and being with the living Christ in the bread and wine. This mystery of faith goes way beyond our intellectual understanding.

Leslie Weatherhead tells of a Methodist friend who attended a Catholic church. After the service, the friend asked one of the worshipers about what happened in the Mass. The old man responded with the following:

> When I come to Mass, sir, I cannot follow what they do up at the altar. I just kneel down and think about Jesus. I think of that last week with His friends and the last supper; how He knelt in agony in Gethsemane; how they arrested Him and all night tortured Him and how He died. . . . I get very near to Jesus then, sir, and when I go home I feel that He comes with me.[1]

When I sit with people who know they are dying, often I ask, "Is there anything I can do for you?" They may just shake their head, they may ask me to pray, or they may ask if they can make a confession. But many times they ask me to bring Holy Communion. They know from their past experiences that this is a Gospel address where they can intimately share in the friendship of Christ. As they go on that lonely journey toward death, they are not craving words or liturgy. Instead, they want to taste the never-ending love of Christ in the bread and wine on their parched, dry lips.

friendship exercise

Remember a time when Communion became a Gospel address where you met Jesus. What made that time so special? Where did it happen? Was it in a church, at home, in a hospital, on a retreat, or someplace else? How did you prepare yourself for that moment? How did you know that you were experiencing Jesus?

The Second Gospel Address—Where Two or Three Gather Together

Sometimes we forget that Jesus enjoyed human friendship. He had deep relationships with many—the beloved disciple, the inner circle of three, the Twelve, the seventy, Mary Magdalene, the women at the cross, and many others. His friendships with Mary, Martha, and their brother Lazarus are notable. When I read of their time together, especially of Lazarus's death, I am touched by the depth of emotion expressed to one another and the obvious mutuality of their friendship. Friendships certainly sustain Jesus during his earthly life. So it comes as little surprise when he says to his followers, "Where two or three gather in my name, there am I with them" (Matt. 18:20, NIV).

These words are often used to underline the importance of coming together in worship or in small groups, but I believe they also refer to the friendships we have with other friends of Jesus. When we open our lives to the friendship of Jesus, he brings his other friends with him. We do not experience a private or exclusive friendship with Jesus. Our friendship with Jesus always combines personal and social dimensions. Jesus' friendship encompasses all those he keeps close to him, and he introduces us to them.

When we reflect on Jesus' many friendships, we notice that they don't all function at the same level of closeness. He clearly seems closer to some individuals than to others. We experience that same variation in our friendships. We may consider some people to be significant soul-friends. Unlike those who constantly drain us or those to whom we relate on a superficial level, deeper friendships sustain, nourish, and grow our faith. They change, comfort, and challenge us. Through them, Christ's risen presence meets us. As such, those friendships represent a Gospel address we need to visit as often as we can.

Experiencing a real soul-friendship today is quite rare. Some years ago, I led a men's retreat with a clinical psychologist friend. During the weekend, we explored four areas of our lives. We looked at our relationships with our fathers, our daily work, our intimate lives, and our friends. I will never forget a comment made by one of the retreatants, an outwardly successful and jovial businessperson. After we had spent the afternoon reflecting on the circles of our friendships, he said, "Today I have realized that I have many acquaintances but no true soul-friends."

A connection resides between our friendship with God and our close friendships with others. One dimension radically affects the other. If we struggle to form significant friendships with those around us, we also will struggle to relate in any depth to our Divine Friend we cannot see. But if we are able to forge meaningful bonds with other men and women on similar faith journeys, we will find our friendship with God constantly refreshed and renewed. I would not be sitting here writing these words were it not for the faithful friendships of a handful of soul-friends along the way. Without them I would have lost my way years ago.

But where can we find these soul-friends? They are all around us if we are willing to look. The following distinctive features help us recognize potential soul-friends:

- They take their friendship with God seriously.
- They have experienced both the mountains and the valleys of the faith-journey.
- They listen attentively without needing to "fix" others.
- They gently confront faults in themselves and in others.
- They do not pretend to have it all together.
- They always point beyond themselves to Christ.

Usually the first step toward a soul-friendship is to seek out a person like this and ask to get together. It can be as simple as saying, "Would you like to meet over coffee and chat about our faith and our lives?"

friendship exercise

Name a soul-friend in your life. What do you value most about this person and your friendship? Does he or she have any of the distinctive features mentioned above? What are other distinctive features of this person? If you cannot think of anyone, consider people in your circle of friendship with whom you could share your joys and struggles in relating to God. Often our search begins with a prayer— *Lord, please lead me to someone with whom I can reflect on my friendship with you.*

The Third Gospel Address— The Least of These

If we wanted to know where Jesus spends the greatest percentage of his time by reading one of the Gospels, the answer would not be too difficult to find. He spends most of his time with people who are struggling in one way or another. He reaches out to the lonely. He includes the excluded. He feeds the hungry. He heals the sick. He brings peace to the chaotic. He comforts the grieving. More often than not, Jesus can be found with those who have been ignored and overlooked.

In his well-known parable of the sheep and the goats, Jesus says that whatever we do to one of the least of these we do to him because Jesus is so close to those who suffer. (See Matthew 25:31-40.) Or to put it the other way around, we meet our Divine Friend in the human cries of those who hurt. This truth is one of the profound mysteries of our faith. Every act of mercy done for someone who suffers is therefore also a direct kindness to Christ who dwells within that individual.

This interconnectedness explains why encounters with people in pain often change us. Almost every day I come into contact with people who are hurting and struggling. These daily encounters with the terminally ill, the unemployed, the economically poor, the divorced, the childless, the bereaved, the forgotten elderly, and other suffering men and women have profoundly affected my understanding and experience of what it means to be a friend of Jesus. The Spirit uses these relationships in the ongoing conversion of my heart and life.

I think of my relationship with Gavin, who died recently. At one time I participated in a ministry called Faith and Life that built friendships with young people with mental disabilities. For almost a year and a half, one Saturday afternoon a month, I would spend time with Gavin for about two hours. At first I didn't really know what to do when we were together. His disabilities precluded conversations, playing games, reading books, and most of the usual activities one can do with a young person. Often I felt very awkward around Gavin and wished the time would go by quickly. My capacity to love him was severely limited.

However, Gavin's capacity to love was much greater than mine. Whenever I arrived, he would come to meet me. Despite my discomfort in his presence, he was at peace in mine. In those moments when I wanted to give up on the friendship, his obvious delight in my company kept me coming back. But the most moving moment in our friendship happened one Sunday night at worship. My preaching didn't seem to be going too well. Gavin was sitting about halfway down the aisle. In the midst of my preaching struggle, he got up, walked to me, and put his arm around my shoulder.

In that holy moment, I realized that my Saturday afternoons with Gavin had become a Gospel address where Christ wanted to meet me. Through our times together, the limits of my love were revealed to me. Gavin challenged me to face my lack of heartfelt compassion and tenderness. I discovered how easily dark feelings of irritability, impatience, and indifference could surface within me, especially when I was not doing what I wanted to do. Acknowledging the darkness in my heart was not easy, but I knew it was necessary if I wanted the Holy Spirit to continue changing my heart of stone into a heart of flesh.

friendship exercise

Think of a time you encountered someone who could be considered "one of the least of these." How did it take place? What feelings were evoked in you through your relationship with this person? How did Christ meet you in that situation? How could you spend more time at this Gospel address?

A special privilege of my daily work is meeting and forming relationships with those who have just begun a friendship with God. Often they will want to know how they can grow in this new friendship. I always advise beginning with the basics—learning how to pray and getting to know Jesus in the Gospels. As we have already seen, we never outgrow these two activities. Additionally, I might counsel on the importance of regularly participating in the worship life of a community that celebrates Communion, of finding soul-friends for the journey, and of opening our lives and hearts to those who suffer. If we go to these three Gospel addresses, Christ will meet us there. As we grow in the divine friendship, we will find ourselves moving from loneliness to meaningful relationships and community.

7

Discerning What Our Friend Wants Us to Do

Once there was a man who loved eating chocolate cake. During Lent he decided to give it up. However, halfway through the Lenten season, he drove past a bakery and saw his favorite cake in the window. He wondered if this was a sign that God wanted him to buy it. So he prayed, "God, if it is really your will that I buy this cake, please provide a space for me to park right outside the shop. Then I will know that you really want me to have it." Evidently on his fifteenth time driving around the block, a parking space finally became available!

I like that story. Often we don't find it easy to discern what God wants us to do. Perhaps that is why we try to force God's hand by demanding a sign of some sort. Yet we know from reading the Bible that God offers to guide us. In one of my favorite New Testament passages, Jesus describes himself as the good shepherd who calls his own sheep by name and leads them. (See John 10:11.) Referring to his relationship with his flock, he says, "When he has brought out all his own, he goes ahead of them, and the sheep follow him because they know his voice" (John 10:4). But how do we discern what our friend wants us to do?

When I first started following Jesus, I received encouragement from those further along on their faith journeys such as the following: "Let God lead you." They would tell me stories of how God had told them what to do when facing difficult decisions. Instead of encouraging me, however, these stories often left me wondering if there was something wrong with my faith because God didn't seem to speak as clearly to me about decisions I had to make. As a result, I often felt confused when it came to deciding what to do, especially in matters about which Jesus or the Bible did not say much.

To make matters worse, these dilemmas often involved choices between two alternatives that were both good options. For example, should I stay in my present job or look for a new one? Get involved in this ministry or that ministry? Marry this person or remain single? Live in this part of the country or somewhere else? Accept this business offer or turn it down? Preach on this subject or some other one? How was I to go about making faithful decisions in accordance with God's will in these sorts of situations when I didn't receive clear guidance from God?

While wrestling with this question I discovered what Jesus most values in our decision-making moments. What do we most value in our human friendships? Our close relationships provide valuable insights into how we can more meaningfully relate to God. When we look at these clues in the light of the person and words of Jesus, they can help us understand the process of discernment in a mature friendship with God.

The Parable of the Unworthy Servant

In Luke 17:7-10, we find a short but startling story that helps us look at faithful decision making in a new way. Jesus describes a servant who does everything his master orders him to do. He exhibits complete obedience. But Jesus interrupts the story with an unexpected question: "Will he thank the servant because he did what he was told to do?" (Luke 17:9, NIV).

Now we don't know for sure how Jesus' listeners would have responded, but my hunch is they would have thought, *Of course the master would thank the servant! He has faithfully done everything he was supposed to do. He has obeyed his master's wishes. What more could one ask from one's servant?* But Jesus turns the conventional thinking of his day upside down as he continues, "So you also, when you have done everything you were told to do, should say, 'We are unworthy servants; we have only done our duty'" (Luke 17:10, NIV).

Jesus' words may surprise us. Just when we thought he would praise the servant for his obedience, he calls him "unworthy." What should we make of this? I know one possibility. If someone who does what he or she is told to do is called unworthy, then the worthy servant must be the one who goes beyond dutiful obedience. In a nutshell, he or she is someone who takes loving initiative and does more than expected. I have learned that what God wants most from us is not mere obedience—not just doing what we are told to do—but a willingness to go beyond and do more.

As we get to know Jesus in the Gospels and study his words, what God generally wants for our lives becomes reasonably clear. Indeed this is one of the first tasks facing us when we enter into friendship with God. We learn that God wants us to love others, to be honest, to serve others, to use our gifts, and to do as much good as we can. These directives from God are absolutely fundamental to making God's dream real in the world. But what does our Divine Friend want us to do in those decisions not explicitly covered by the general teaching of Jesus? This parable reminded me of what Jesus values most—a readiness to take the initiative and discern what decisions will best express our love for him. He wants us to move beyond dutiful obedience into the world of loving initiative.

Beyond Dutiful Obedience

When talking about going beyond dutiful obedience, I do not want to downplay the importance of practical obedience to Jesus. There is nothing wrong in wanting to do everything Jesus tells us to do. However, for Jesus this still remains the attitude of the unworthy servant. As Dallas Willard points out, this frame of mind "severely limits spiritual growth, when measured against the possibilities of a life of free-hearted collaboration with Jesus and his friends in the Kingdom of the Heavens."[1] Learning how to exercise loving initiative freely when making decisions is crucial to our growing friendship with God as well as to the healthy development of our own character.

To explain, I offer the following illustration: As parents, we give our children exact instructions about how they should behave and what actions are appropriate and expected. We are pleased when they do what we tell them. One day, without our asking, they do something extra, something special. We are delighted in this development. They are growing up and beginning to take initiative in expressing their love for others. Even if they don't do it perfectly, we recognize that they are expressing their love. Hopefully the joy they see in our faces will encourage many more actions of loving initiative!

Friend and colleague Wessel Bentley tells a wonderful story on his blog. As he was driving home with his five-year-old son, Matthew, Wessel said, to no one in particular, "I'm really hungry." When they got home, Wessel went to his study to work. A few minutes later his son appeared at the door holding a tray with hot coffee and warm toast. In that moment, Wessel's heart was flooded with appreciation, gratitude, and love. His son had taken action without being asked. He had sensed his father's need and taken loving initiative to do something about it.

Wise parents know that children need space to grow into their God-given potential. Therefore, these parents will give their children increasing opportunity to make their own decisions as they grow up. Children cannot grow into competent, responsible adults if they are always told what to do. Their character develops, both for better and for worse, as they make their own choices. Reality slowly teaches them that, although they may be free to do anything they want, they are not free to choose the consequences of their actions. Within the framework of personal decision making and experiencing the effects of their choices, children grow into responsible adults.

Now we can understand why God does not always tell us what to do. God wants us to grow into maturity. In effect God says, "What I want for your life is that you will shape your own path in creative, responsible, and life-giving ways. As your Divine Friend, I am very interested in what you want to do and the decisions you will make. If there is anything I want you to do, I will make it clear to you. Otherwise, take initiative and seek to make decisions that are in tune with my dream. This is how you will grow into the person I want you to be. And, above all, always know my Spirit is with you."

Let's now explore practical ways that we can move beyond dutiful obedience in our decision making. As we have seen, doing only what God tells us to do is the attitude of the unworthy servant. God wants us to grow into the wonderful freedom of becoming mature children of our Heavenly Parent. We please God when we show loving initiative in the divine friendship. But what does that mean in practice when we are facing choices that the Bible does not discuss? How do we make decisions that correspond with what our Friend wants for our lives?

friendship exercise

Think of a time when someone did something special for you without your having asked. How did you feel to be on the receiving end of this action? How did this person know you would value what he or she did for you? In what way was he or she in tune with your heart? How would your reaction have differed if you had asked this person to do what he or she did for you? What does this experience reveal to you about how you can relate to your Divine Friend?

How Do We Make Faithful Decisions?

When facing a decision that the counsel of scripture does not cover, we must first discuss it with God. We do this with the confidence and expectancy that God will plainly communicate with us anything God wants to say and that our Divine Friend will not purposefully confuse us. I usually offer the following prayer: *God, I want to be faithful to your dream for my life and for your world in this situation. Please help me. Help me to hear what you are saying to me. Speak through the people who cross my path, the circumstances in which I find myself, my moments of reading the scriptures, or whatever way you choose.*

Once I have sought God's guidance in this way, I move forward with my life as usual, paying careful attention to what happens within me and around me. If I am drawn strongly to one course of action, I make a mental note of it. Later I will think more deeply about it and perhaps talk about it with a trusted soul-friend. If I experience any unease or uncertainty, I will ask for God's confirmation. Over the years I have followed this practice with all kinds of decisions ranging from ordinary ones, such as how to respond in a family conflict, to bigger ones, such as whether to accept a job offer overseas.

I have become convinced that if God wants to say anything about a decision we face, God will say it clearly. God does not mumble! If we are facing a certain issue, we can know almost beyond a doubt what God wants us to do. We remember David and his dramatic encounter with God just after he has become king. The Philistines have attacked Israel, and David asks God for guidance. "Shall I go up against the Philistines?" David asks (1 Chron. 14:10). God replies, "Go up, and I will give them into your hand" (1 Chron. 14:10).

However, God does not always tell us what to do. We may pray about a particular decision and still feel unsure about what to do. No thought stands out clearly with those characteristics that we link with God's voice. In such cases, we need to remind ourselves of what God values most in the divine friendship and assume that God wants us to take loving initiative and to go about actively discerning what to do. This involves clarifying what we most want to do for God and running it through what I call "God's tuning fork test."

God's Tuning Fork

Recently I worshiped in a church with a choir but no instrumental music. At the beginning of the service, the choir conductor got up and struck the tuning fork against a table. The choir members silenced themselves, listened attentively, and then hummed together. To get the right note, the conductor struck the tuning fork against the table again. Once more the choir members responded by humming together the note they had heard. After a third attempt, the conductor was satisfied. They were all in tune and ready to sing.

We could say that God has struck the earth with the tuning fork of Jesus. More than anyone else who has ever lived, Jesus was a human being perfectly in tune with God's will. When we listen carefully to the message of his words and deeds, his death and resurrection, we hear the notes of God's grace-saturated intention for our world to be healed. Jesus helps us to catch the tune of God's hope-filled melody that good will overcome evil, truth will overcome deception, and community will overcome disunity. Above all, Jesus helps us hear the music of God's dream that we will learn to live lovingly as friends in harmony with God and one another. This is how we use God's tuning fork test. We discern which of our deepest desires resonates more with God's tuning fork than others. Those desires that echo Jesus' heart usually possess the following characteristics:

- They draw us in the direction of a fuller, more creative life.
- They engage us more personally in the suffering of others.
- They nourish our lives and the lives of others.
- They open up fresh possibilities for relationship.
- They invite us into deeper loving.
- They draw us into deeper friendship with God.

But we need to look for one critical characteristic. Those much wiser than I am suggest that when our wants genuinely resonate with the heart of our Divine Friend, we will experience a sense of calm and peace when we decide to put them into action. When they are not in tune with God's will, we will feel agitated, anxious, and unsettled. Paul encourages the Colossian Christ-followers to allow the peace of Christ to guide them in their decisions. (See Colossians 3:15.) To put it plainly, when God leads and guides us, we experience a profound sense of peace about the decision we are making.

Obviously, we need to watch out for a false sense of peace, which may derive from one of several sources. A false peace can come from simply wanting to escape a conflict-ridden situation, from trying to avoid a necessary hardship, or from not wanting to move out of a familiar or comfortable space. False peace is superficial and temporary, offering quick relief when facing difficult choices. The peace given by God's Spirit endures through all the ups and downs of our more fleeting emotions and moods. It does not guarantee the absence of trouble; rather, it produces a strong conviction, even in the midst of trouble, that God is with us and we are not alone. For this reason, an inner joy, serenity, and aliveness usually accompany the peace given by the Holy Spirit, no matter what is happening around us.

But what if none of our desires stands out strongly with God's peace? Again we should take loving initiative. We do this by thinking through the issue, making the best decision we can, and offering it to God with all the love of our hearts. The steps in that process include reflecting on the pros and cons, trying to weigh the consequences of each choice, requesting the counsel of others, and taking full responsibility for whatever decision we finally make. We act on our decision, and we trust God with the outcome.

I am a few years away from formal retirement. How do I best prepare myself for that moment of transition? Will I continue my work that I'm doing now after retirement, or do I need to prepare myself for a change and new tasks? Both options are good, but neither Jesus nor the Bible directly addresses my possibility. I want to be faithful to what God wants for my life. As I think about these questions, I find it useful to get in touch with my deepest desires regarding my future and to apply God's tuning fork test. I then ask myself in God's presence, *Which of my desires leaves me with the deepest peace?*

friendship exercise

What decisions are you facing right now? Take a few moments to focus on one area of decision making where God has not made it clear about what you should do. Assume that God wants you to move beyond a dutiful obedience and take loving initiative. What would you like to do in relation to the issue you are facing? Apply God's tuning fork test. Would it lead you toward a more abundant life? Would it increase your faith, hope, and love? As you think about following through on what you want to do, what are your feelings? Do you sense a steady peacefulness or unease? When you interpret and evaluate your different choices in this way, the Spirit will lead you toward healthy decisions in your friendship with God.

8

Facing Our Fears
with Our Friend

All of us, to some degree, know what it means to be scared. Each day brings some kind of fear into our hearts and minds, whether it is fear of failure or success, fear of people or of death, fear of the past or of the future. Not many can honestly claim to live without fear. I know this from personal experience as well as from many years of listening to people share their stories. We always seem to find something to fear. At times, we may even fear of God.

Fear can sabotage our lives. To begin with, fear is accompanied by negative health effects. Our hearts begin to race, our breathing becomes heavier, our mouths go dry, and tension spreads throughout our bodies. Emotionally, fear causes us to feel down, even despairing and depressed, stealing the sparkle from our lives. The relational consequences can be equally crippling. Fear builds walls between people, prevents our connecting with others, and turns us into hoarders rather than givers. Most tragically of all, fear undermines our friendship with God.

Earlier we explored God's dream for our lives and our world. I boldly said that God longs passionately for a world where we live in friendship with God, with each other, and with the rest of creation. God wants us to live in tune with this dream wherever we find ourselves—in our homes, at our places of work, in our communities. Few forces work against this dream more than fear. Fear poisons relationships between neighbors, deepens divisions along racial and economic lines, and fosters hatred between nations. Almost more than anything else, fear sabotages our desire to make God's dream a greater reality in our midst.

The Bible speaks about the negative power of fear. The phrase "fear not" is spoken many times. Clearly, the biblical writers believed fear undermined our ability to work for God's dream. We now face the challenge of discovering how to put these words about not fearing into practice. How can living more consciously in friendship with God reduce our levels of fear?

Acknowledging Our Fears

As we explore this question, let us keep in mind the Gospel story of Jesus and his frightened friends on the boat on the Sea of Galilee. (See Mark 4:35-41.) The first thing that stands out for me is how the disciples acknowledge their fears. When the storm gets worse and the waves begin to break over the boat, the disciples face their fear head-on. They do not pretend to be courageous, attempt to mask their terror, or try to cover up their fear. They admit it openly, honestly, and directly. Cold, wet, and exhausted from rowing all night, they face the fear that haunts them. They don't want to drown.

Mark's story gets me wondering about those fears that keep us from giving our hearts to God. What fears stop us from living in friendship with God and with one another? This Gospel story invites us to be honest with ourselves and to acknowledge those fears.

Naming our fears honestly is not as straightforward or simple as it may sound. Most fear-ridden people don't usually think they are afraid. Unless their fears are directly linked to something external—snakes, darkness, or public speaking—many people held captive by fear may deny their own fearfulness. But when we live in denial, we can easily end up in bondage to what we refuse to acknowledge. This is why we need to look honestly at our fears. If we don't, they could end up controlling us.

The following four fears aren't discussed often: fear of knowing ourselves; fear of being vulnerable; fear of the cry of the poor, the suffering, and the desperate; and fear of God. Each of these fears can prevent us from sharing wholeheartedly and freely in God's dream. Once we understand the fears, we can ask ourselves whether any of these fears are present in our lives.

Fear of Knowing Ourselves

Facing our real selves can feel uncomfortable. Each of us is a mixture of strength and weakness, light and shadow, good and evil. We tend to let others see only the positive sides of our personalities, and we hide the more unwelcome truths—perhaps even from ourselves. We can go through our entire lives showing off our flattering public images, refusing to face the shadowy parts of our inner lives. Naming these hidden dimensions of who we are humiliates the ego. For this reason, getting to know ourselves can be so scary.

Fear can easily sabotage God's dream. We form real friendships only when we are willing to be authentic. This is true for both our friendship with God and with each other. When we only present the more acceptable parts of our personalities, we rob ourselves of experiencing genuine friendship. God longs to meet us in the depths of our being, especially in those broken parts we consider unacceptable and sinful. When we experience God's unconditional friendship and love in these broken places, we can find the courage to let others know who we really are.

Fear of Being Vulnerable

Recently I sat with someone who had brought great pain to his family by hiding from them the financial struggles he was having with his business. Eventually, when his company was forced to go into liquidation, he had to come clean with his wife and children. They were devastated by the loss of the family business but even more so by the many years of deception. As he and I reflected on what he had done, I asked him what had made it so difficult for him to share his struggles. He answered simply, "I don't find it easy to be vulnerable."

He is not alone. Many of us keep our vulnerability and weaknesses hidden. Why? Perhaps, as I pointed out in the previous section, we find it too hard to let go of our public image that says we have it all together. Perhaps a rough childhood necessitated defense mechanisms, and letting them go frightens us. Maybe we have built a high wall around our hearts, protecting ourselves from hurt and also keeping others away from who we really are. The list goes on. Whatever the reason, our fear of being vulnerable prevents us from knowing authentic friendship with God and others.

Fear of the Poor, the Suffering, and the Desperate

While walking down a street one day, a man asking for money approached me. When I asked him why, he began to describe his recent release from the hospital. He showed me the dirty, red bandages around his leg, his prescription for pain medication, and the card showing the date for his next appointment. He said he needed money for food and taxi fare to get home to see his family. Suddenly, I realized that if this conversation went on for much longer, I would feel obliged to get involved even more. I got scared, gave him some cash, and quickly moved on.

Later I thought about my fear in this encounter. The man was in great need and had much anguish. But what did I fear? Was I afraid of getting involved in the man's life? Was I scared of being used or manipulated? Was I fearful of being seen talking with someone in poverty? Was the meeting I needed to attend more pressing than the suffering right in front of me? (Was not the parable of the good Samaritan about this very issue?) As I thought about these questions, I was aware of how my fear of responding to the human cries around me stops me from living out God's dream for the world.

Fear of God

The Bible seems to offer mixed messages about fear. It repeatedly tells us not to fear; on the other hand, we are also told to fear God. We might consider the following well-known proverb: "The fear of the LORD is the beginning of wisdom" (Prov. 9:10). What are we to do? Are we supposed to fear God or not fear God? This passage can quickly bring to the surface negative feelings we may have as a result of a distorted picture of God.

Personally, I am convinced that we are not meant to be frightened of God. When we are told to fear God in the Bible, we are being invited into a respectful reverence for God. The reality of the Divine Presence in and around us always evokes a profound sense of awe. When reflections about friendship with God degenerate into a superficial "Jesus is my buddy" way of relating, we have missed the point. And yet, if fear dominates our relationship with God, that fear must be faced. Otherwise, it will keep us from playing our part in God's dream of friendship with us.

friendship exercise

If any of the fears described draw your attention to fears of your own, take time to acknowledge them. Don't avoid them. Face these fears honestly, and name them for what they are. Remember that often what we refuse to face has the greatest potential to hold power over us. Psychologist David G. Benner points out, "To deny the reality of fears is not to know ourselves, and then we risk becoming possessed by that which we refuse to face."[1]

Of course, this exercise will not be easy. You may ask yourself, *What allows me to acknowledge my fears now?* To answer this, I will remind you that you are not doing it alone. You are naming your fears as God's beloved friend. When you face your fear in the knowledge that you are loved, accepted, and forgiven by God in Jesus Christ, the fears' power over you diminishes. As you learned from the disciples in the boat, acknowledging your fears can open your life to the miracle of God's loving care. The writer of First John explains what happens when your life is covered with the perfect love of God— "There is no fear in love, but perfect love casts out fear" (4:18).

Telling Our Divine Friend

During the storm in Mark 4, the disciples tell Jesus about their fear. They go to where he is sleeping and cry out, "Teacher, do you not care that we are perishing?" (Mark 4:38). This short sentence reveals a lot about their anxiety. They are scared of the windstorm and the rain. They are terrified the boat might sink. They are frightened of losing their lives. They are worried that Jesus will do nothing to help them. Naming their fear in his presence eventually leads them into a wonderful experience of Jesus' love and power.

This Gospel moment encourages us to bring our fears to the God whom Jesus reveals. No matter the fear, we can tell our Divine Friend about it. Like the experience of the disciples, such admissions can lead to a powerful encounter with God. We too may find that the winds and storms blowing in our lives begin to calm. Even more than this, our friendship with God will become more intimate and more alive. And then we can enter into the transforming dimension of friendship with God.

How does this happen? We can draw parallels from human friendship. When fear paralyzes us, we may acknowledge our fear inwardly, but it would be quite another matter to share it with a close friend. Something significant happens when we do. A stronger closeness develops between us. We no longer feel we are on our own. We get a sense of relief after having put our fear into words. We will probably listen much more attentively to what our friend is saying to us after we have opened up to him or her. Our mind is no longer totally absorbed in our fear.

A similar change occurs when we share our deep fears with God. Because we are being honest about what is happening in our lives, we perceive a greater reality in our friendship with our Divine Friend. A richer intimacy blooms in our life together. We feel more connected. We are not as afraid of being alone, being abandoned, or being unloved as we were before. We let the loving and powerful presence of God penetrate our very depths. We are more open to hearing God's voice.

I do this sharing very simply. I write down whatever I am afraid of, and then I also tell God about it in words. I may fear illness, the future, the loss of someone I love, the negative thoughts of others, my own death, or something described above. I name this fear in the presence of the risen Christ knowing that it does not have the power to separate me from him. I ask him to help me face it, overcome it, and take whatever action is needed. Although going through this process seldom takes away my fear completely, when I bring it to God in this way, the fear becomes less ominous and more manageable.

Sometimes we also need to share our fears with a human friend. We go to someone we trust—a person who will listen, who stands outside the influence of our fears, and who can be the face of Christ for us. A friend like this often takes away the burden of loneliness that accompanies our biggest fears. As our friend's heart touches our heart, strength is imparted, and we grow in friendship. Are we surprised? No, for Jesus tells us, "Where two or three are gathered in my name, I am there among them" (Matt. 18:20).

friendship exercise

Take one fear you wrote down in the previous Friendship Exercise and tell God about it in your own words. Tell God how this fear affects you. This exercise is not about giving information to God; rather, you are seeking to grow your friendship with God. Sharing with God in this way gives God greater access to those fears with which you struggle.

Living Beyond Fear

The Gospel story of the disciples in the boat ends with Jesus challenging them to greater faith. Jesus asks them, "Why are you afraid? Have you still no faith?" (Mark 4:40). I have thought a lot about this challenge. To be sure, these men already have faith *in* Jesus. They have left everything—their families, their jobs—to follow Jesus. They have already exercised a remarkable degree of faith in Jesus, certainly a great deal more than most of us will in our lifetimes. But what they need most in their friendship with God is the faith *of* Jesus.

Let's imagine the Gospel story one last time. The dark, angry storm on the sea, the howling wind, the rough waves—they all symbolize those monster-fears that threaten God's dream for this world. The boat in which Jesus and his disciples travel is in danger of sinking. The disciples are terrified, but Jesus is so confident in his Father's care that he falls asleep in the back of the boat. When they cry out to him in their understandable fear, he asks them, "Why are you afraid? Have you still no faith?"

Clearly Jesus possesses a faith in his Father that his disciples do not. He knows this is his Father's world. He knows the universe is permeated with, bathed in, and filled with God's presence. He knows nothing can separate him from his Father. He lives confidently in this trust and knowledge. He knows that while his intimate oneness with his Father won't protect him from torture and crucifixion, he does not need to live in fear. This is the faith the disciples lack. Not so much faith *in* Jesus but the faith *of* Jesus. They need Jesus' faith in his Father.

How can we begin to develop this kind of faith? Like the disciples, we will make a journey in our friendship with Jesus. As we get to know him—opening our minds to his ideas about God, putting his words into practice—we gradually will grow from having faith *in* him to having *his* faith. We will realize that we are never alone in this God-permeated and God-bathed universe. We know that nothing in this world, not even death, can ever separate us from God's presence in Jesus Christ. As we keep company with Jesus in this intimate way, we will begin to share his faith in the living God, and we too start to live beyond fear.

Imagine the freedom we would have if we could live beyond fear—the freedom to be ourselves without any need to impress or perform, the freedom to relate to others honestly, openly, and non-defensively, the freedom to open our hearts to those who suffer and are desperate, the freedom to befriend our death and enjoy each present moment, and above all, the freedom to surrender our lives fully to the intimate friendship that God passionately longs to have with each one of us.

Consider these words from Scottish philosopher John Macmurray, quoted in William A. Barry, SJ's book *God's Passionate Desire*, that invite us into the faith that Jesus had in his heavenly Parent.

> The maxim of illusory religion runs: "Fear not; trust in God and he will see that none of the things you fear will happen to you"; that of real religion, on the contrary, is "Fear not; the things that you are afraid of are quite likely to happen to you, but they are nothing to be afraid of."[2]

friendship exercise

I certainly don't live without fear. If you want to respond to Jesus' challenge to grow in faith, the best way is to keep company with Jesus. Take part in this experiment for the next twenty-four hours. Acknowledge Jesus' presence when you wake up. Invite him into every activity you undertake during the day. Ask him for help and guidance in your daily tasks. See him in the people you meet, especially those in pain. If you do this for one day, you will be able to do it for the next day as well. As you practice his presence in this way, trusting that his Spirit is with you, you will come to share Jesus' faith in his Father more and more. As you learned from the frightened disciples in the boat, it is faith that helps you live beyond fear.

9

Asking Our Friend
the Hardest Question

I remember clearly the first funeral service I performed. The Methodist Church had appointed me as a probationer minister in a rural area of South Africa called the Transkei. I was to work there for a year, gain some practical ministry experience, and begin my six years of training. During the first week in Mthatha, I received a phone call from a young father. He asked if I would bury his still-born child. The mother was still in the hospital recovering from the complications of giving birth, and he wanted me to conduct a simple burial service.

That was my first personal encounter with the raw grief that comes when we have been treated unfairly by life. I still recall walking across the graveyard with the father as he carried the little white coffin. We knelt together in the dust to place it in the ground. He sobbed uncontrollably and asked me the hardest question of all: "Why did God allow this to happen?"

When terrible things happen, we all ask this question. It may be the death of a child; the onset of a crippling disease; a tragic accident; the loss of sight, hearing, or memory; the collapse of a business; or something else that brings terrible anguish. While circumstances differ, a common thread links these painful losses: a sense of overwhelming and unjust suffering. How do we reconcile such devastating events with a God who passionately longs to be friends with us? What good is God's friendship when God allows these things to happen?

We ask the question too when we have been sinned against. Recently a young, married woman, her life scarred by years of horrific childhood abuse, asked, "If God really loved me, why didn't he stop my father from molesting me?" Even when we are not directly affected, we ask this question when we witness evil at work. Not long ago, a four-year-old boy in a nearby community was dragged to his death through the streets for four kilometers by a car in a botched hijacking attempt. Just contemplating the indescribable suffering caused to this child and his family is painful.

Why does God allow bad things to happen? When we add the suffering caused by natural disasters, the question becomes almost impossible to engage. Scientists help us understand why events like earthquakes and tsunamis occur. These explanations allow us to take whatever preventable measures we can to lessen the possibilities of human suffering. But we remain unable to answer the question of why a loving God, who desires us into existence for the sake of friendship, allows human life to be harmed or wiped out in these ways.

Let's look at this question through the eyes of Jesus. We find no easy answer, if indeed an answer exists at all. Certainly I don't have a satisfactory answer to why a God who is all-loving and all-powerful allows rape, abuse, disease, birth abnormalities, natural disasters, and so forth to happen. But I hope our reflections will provide a solid place where we can stand, especially when we find ourselves overwhelmed by human suffering and tragedy.

God Does Not Cause Our Suffering

In chapter 3, we explored the bottom line of the Christian faith. If we want to know what God is like, we can look at Jesus. Jesus reveals God's heart, God's character, and God's will. If we want to know how God feels about human suffering, the best approach we can take is look at Jesus' response to it. Not once does Jesus say to someone suffering, "This is what God wants for your life" or " It's God's will, so just accept it." Not once! Every time Jesus encounters human pain and suffering, he responds in positive ways. He understands that human suffering is completely alien to the dream that God has for this world.

We need to grasp this truth. The God who wants to be friends with us, the God whom we meet in Jesus Christ, does not cause suffering. God does not send leukemia to a little baby or manipulate a tragic accident to teach us a lesson or wipe out a community because of disobedience. Such events and circumstances are characteristics of the broken and bent nature of the world in which we live. While we cannot argue with the mysterious reality that such things have been allowed to happen, Jesus gives us this blessed assurance: God does not cause our suffering.

When we are unsure of this fact, we will sometimes make unhelpful comments to those who are hurting. A few months ago I performed a funeral for a young man. In the program, the funeral parlor printed the following sentence from scripture: *"He gives, and he takes away."* (See Job 1:21.) These words from the lips of Job are not good theology for such a time as a funeral. They are bad theology. When Job says those words after he loses his children, his health, and his wealth, he has not yet understood the true nature of his tragedy or God's will for his life, which is always for good and not harm. God is not the author of sin, evil, or suffering. A more appropriate Bible verse for a funeral might be Hebrews 13:5: "I will never leave or forsake you."

William Barclay, well-known writer of commentaries on the New Testament, sometimes upset readers with his biblical interpretations.

When his daughter and her fiancé tragically drowned in a yacht-
ing accident, he received an anonymous letter that read, "Dear Dr.
Barclay, I know now why God killed your daughter; it was to save
her from being corrupted by your heresies."[1] Not having the letter
writer's address, Barclay was unable to respond. In his autobiography he wrote the following:

> If I had had that writer's address, I would have written back,
> not in anger—the inevitable blaze of anger was over in a
> flash—but in pity, and I would have said to him, as John
> Wesley said to someone: "Your God is my devil." The day my
> daughter was lost at sea there was sorrow in the heart of God.[2]

When we look at suffering through the eyes of Jesus, we find
comfort and assurance. He helps us to know that God does not
cause suffering but is deeply grieved by it. We do not say to ourselves in moments of suffering and tragedy, *God did this to me, and
there must be some reason* or *It's God's will.* No. Our Divine Friend
only wants what is good for us—what is true, beautiful, loving, and
life-giving.

When we begin to understand that God does not want us to
suffer, we find ourselves called to do whatever we can to relieve
human suffering. If suffering is not caused by God and is alien to
God's dream, then as God's friends we need to do as much as we
can to help those who suffer. Earlier I emphasized the importance
of looking outward in the same direction as Jesus. While we cannot
take on all the suffering around us, we can look outward and ask
God, *Where do you want me to work with you in easing the suffering
of others?* When we offer justice and mercy to those who suffer, we
live in tune with God's dream for our hurting world.

friendship exercise

How do you wrestle with the question of why God allows suffering? Give some time to your own personal reflections around this

question. How does the question, "Why does God allow human suffering?" affect you? When have you found yourself asking that question? What do you say to those who have experienced suffering? What unhelpful comments were said to you in times of suffering? What would it mean for you to look at suffering through the eyes of Jesus?

Whose Fault Is It Then?

In the Gospel of John, we find the story of a man born blind. The disciples come to Jesus and ask, "Rabbi, who sinned, this man or his parents, that he was born blind?" (John 9:2). The disciples presume some connection between the man's disability and previous sin. But whose sin is it? The disciples are adamant that either the blind man or his parents must have acted wrongly for him to be born without sight. Now they want Jesus to reveal the guilty party.

This kind of thinking is a popular way of trying to work out why God allows suffering. We believe in God's justice so if someone is suffering, he or she must have deserved it. Sickness, failure, and broken relationships could signify sin or wrongdoing in our lives. Therefore, God must be punishing us for some previous sin. In this way, we try to maintain the belief that God must be fair. On the other side of this coin, we assume that if we have success, health, good families, and careers, God has blessed us for the good lives we have lived.

Jesus responds to his disciples' thinking. Being born blind does not mean that the man has sinned. Nor does it mean that his parents are bad. Something much deeper, much more mysterious is going on in this particular situation. Jesus responds, "He was born blind so that God's works might be revealed in him" (John 9:3). Through his words, Jesus sheds some light on the dark mystery of human suffering and pain. Our pain and suffering, such as this man's blindness, are the raw materials in and through which the Father works to make all things new.

While this story does not fully answer our question, it does affirm a hopeful insight we can keep in mind: God is always at work in our lives in every moment, in every situation, in every relationship—no matter how chaotic or painful it may be. At the heart of everything in our universe, our loving and active Divine Friend seeks to bring hope and life where suffering and pain exist. For the most part we cannot understand in the present moment just how God may be working. But we recognize an invitation into deeper trust that I will explore at the end of this chapter.

Having affirmed Jesus' refusal to connect all suffering with sin, we must acknowledge that disobedience to God's way causes some suffering. Our actions have consequences for ourselves and for others. As my children grew up, I would often say to them, "We are free to do anything we want, but we are not free to choose the consequences." God gave us the Ten Commandments, which are, at the very least, God's invitation to life at its best. God is not being a spoilsport. Instead, God offers the moral foundations that lead toward human life as it is meant to be.

When we act out of selfishness, greed, apathy, lust, or other destructive patterns of behavior, we may well meet with terrible suffering, both in our own lives and in the lives of those around us. I know this from personal experience. There have been times of real pain in my marriage. Some of this heartache was caused by my sinful patterns of behavior—moments when I withdrew from Debbie into a sulky coldness, when I was not honest about what I had been thinking and feeling, when I failed to be there for her in supportive ways. I cannot blame God for this pain; I caused it myself.

friendship exercise

Identify a destructive behavior or emotion that has caused pain in your life. Some of your suffering may come from frustration at things not going your way, feelings of inferiority, an inability to give love or receive love, a refusal to forgive, unfaithfulness to your partner, or dishonesty. Whatever it may be, remember that God meets you in your pain and hurt. If you are able to bring this suffering to your Divine Friend and acknowledge your part in it, you will move toward a greater wholeness in your life.

God Weeps with Us

As we remember the bottom line of our faith—God has come to us in Jesus of Nazareth—we know we can look at Jesus' actions and see God at work. Let us therefore look once more at Jesus' response to those hurting around him. The God we meet in Jesus is no stranger to suffering. Our Divine Friend shares our suffering intimately, enters our grief, and weeps with us.

One of my favorite Gospel stories recounts when Jesus' friends Mary and Martha call him to their home because their brother, Lazarus, is ill. (See John 11:1-44.) When Jesus arrives, having delayed his coming, Lazarus has already died. Mary approaches Jesus, and he sees that she and many others are weeping. He is so deeply moved and troubled that he begins to weep as well. The Greek words used in this passage suggest that Jesus shudders, is in anguish, and gives out a loud cry of pain.

This image of Jesus weeping takes us deep into the suffering heart of our God. He is not weeping because Lazarus has died. After all, he knows that he is going to bring him back to life. He cries when he sees the pain of Mary and the others around her in tears. He does not condemn them for their tears. He does not tell them to cheer up. He does not tell them that everything will be okay. Rather, Jesus enters their grief, shares it with them, and weeps with them. In this moment, we see the Holy One whom we worship sharing in our pain and weeping with us.

What then are we to do in our times of anguish and pain? To begin, we must refuse to pretend or to cover up our real feelings. We need not experience guilt over negative feelings we may have toward God. We can weep, grieve, or even rage against God. But

we can weep and grieve and rage with hope because we know our
Friend weeps with us, shares our grief, and understands our rage.
More than this, we also know that the God who has come to us in
Jesus is the same God who raises Jesus from the grave. Through the
crucified and risen Messiah, God whispers to us in our suffering,
"Neither evil nor suffering nor death will have the final word. The
last word belongs to me. It is the word of resurrection and life."

Resurrection and life—Jesus helps us to stand on these promises. Knowing that God does not cause our suffering but weeps with
us in these moments does not answer all our questions, take away
our pain, lessen our sorrow, or relieve our grief. Nor does it silence
that dark voice tempting us with the thought, *You are on your own.
You cannot trust God. God does not care. God is not good.* But with
God's help, we can look at our suffering through the eyes of Jesus.
When we do this, we find ourselves able to say, "Divine Friend, help
me to trust you. I refuse to believe anything bad about you. Rather,
I will trust that you weep with us. Indeed, I will trust that you will
make all things new."

friendship exercise

Take some time to talk with God friend-to-friend about your sadness and pain. Keep in your mind the image of the God who suffers
with you, who shares your grief, who understands your pain. Tell
God about your feelings—they may be anger, disappointment, frustration, or distrust—and tell the details of your heartache as fully as
you can. Ask God to be true to you friendship. Speak openly with
God about what you are thinking, even if you believe God already
knows. This conversation is not intended to give God information
but to grow a friendship with God in the midst of suffering.

10

Blessing Others as Our Friend Has Blessed Us

A short expression often pops up among families and friends. It consists of three simple words we use when a friend sneezes, when we say good-bye, when we sign an e-mail, or when we send a card. We may use the words in conversation with strangers on a train or in a shop or in a hospital. Sadly, however, we usually say these words without thinking much about what we mean. These words are *God bless you*.

Blessing is a major theme among the friends of God in the Bible. We should not be surprised. The God we meet on the pages of scripture is constantly blessing. For example, the first thing God does in the creation story after creating a man and a woman in God's own image is to bless them. From that first blessing onward, God blesses people in so many different ways and in so many different places that it is impossible to reduce blessing to a simple formula or technique. However, and I want to emphasize this, God's blessing is never an end in and of itself. We are always blessed so that we can be blessings to others.

Let's consider the covenant God made with Abraham, who was called God's friend. (See Genesis 12:1-3 and 2 Chronicles 20:7.) In effect, God says two things to Abraham, who at that time is named Abram, that we must not separate. First, God promises him, "I will bless you" (Gen. 12:2). Second, God assures him, "You will be a blessing" (Gen. 12:2). Here we see how Abraham is both blessed by God and called to become the ancestor of a people who will bring God's blessing to all the people of the earth. This pattern is typical of how God's dream unfolds throughout the Bible. God chooses to bless others through those who have received divine blessing.

We have been exploring how God blesses us in Jesus Christ through the gift of divine friendship. We have seen that in our friendship with God we receive many profound blessings. We discover that we are loved, accepted, and forgiven. We enter into a conversational relationship with the Creator of the universe. We inherit a new family of brothers and sisters. We are given new hearts and new minds. We find our unique places in God's dream for this world. Most importantly, we come to know that we are never alone. Blessings abound!

When talking about these blessings, I like to focus on the different ways we have been gifted with the *presence* of God rather than the *presents* of God. I do this for two reasons. First, others may feel excluded when we talk about our blessings. This happens when we talk of our blessings primarily as *presents* from God. While we want to thank God for those good things we have, we need to be careful how we express ourselves. Many people do not feel blessed, and the pain we cause others with thoughtless talk about God's blessings can be deep.

Second, as friends of Jesus our greatest contentment and joy lies in our experience of God's *presence* and not just in the *presents* we receive. As Paul tells us in his letter to the Romans, we are blessed to be more than conquerors. (See Romans 8:37.) Even when we go through painful times of desolation and darkness, nothing "will be able to separate us from the love of God in Christ Jesus our Lord" (Rom. 8:39). It is the *presence* of our Divine Friend that strengthens us in weakness, comforts us in heartache, and accompanies us in our loneliness. Our greatest blessings are always found within the conscious, personal, and intimate friendship that we have with the living God.

friendship exercise

Take time now to reflect on some of the blessings you have received in your friendship with God. In what ways have you recently experienced God blessing you? Often you receive these blessings—welcome, gratitude, encouragement, and love—through moments of human interaction. These moments bless you because they serve as gentle yet solid reminders of the presence of your Divine Friend who loves you and longs for you to receive a blessing. I encourage you to do this exercise as often as you can. Notice, receive, and treasure your blessings from God. As the song goes, "Count your blessings, name them one by one. . . . And it will surprise you what the Lord has done."

How to Bless Others

Like Abraham, we are blessed to be a blessing. Something goes painfully wrong when the cycle of God's blessing stops with us. When we accept God's extravagant proposal of divine friendship, we become part of a family that God has been forming over the centuries to bless the world. Learning how to bless others makes God's dream real. But how do we begin? I have observed three types of blessings that all God's friends are invited to practice. They work together closely, and seldom does one occur without the others. The blessings are as follows: the blessing of seeing, the blessing of presence, and the blessing of words.

The Blessing of Seeing

Miracles of blessing happen when we start to see those around us. I have always been struck by the fact that the first miracle in the book of Acts takes place after Peter and John *look* at a man who was born without the use of his legs. (See Acts 3:1-10.) This instance is not the first time they have seen him. The man's friends place him outside the Temple every day to beg. But his suffering has become part of the unnoticed landscape. Soon after the Holy Spirit had come upon Peter and John, the two disciples see this man and become aware of him as a fellow human being, a person whom God loves, someone whom God wants to bless through them. We bring God's blessing by learning to see each other.

Each of us has a profound need to be seen that begins early in our childhood. We have all heard children repeatedly call out to their parents, "Watch me!" I remember watching my son play cricket in primary school. He was a very keen fast-bowler. Whenever he bowled someone out, the first thing he did was turn toward the bleachers where I sat. He wanted to know if I had seen him or not. He needed to know he was not invisible.

Adults are also blessed by being seen. When persons genuinely sees us, it is as if they say, "Your life has dignity and infinite worth. I am interested in your well-being. You matter to me." God's blessing flows into our lives when we see ourselves through the eyes of another person in this way. There is little doubt that, as Ronald Rolheiser puts it, "To see someone or be seen by someone else, in a positive light, is a blessing."[1]

Not to be seen is to feel cursed. The other day an elderly person expressed her pain in this way: "People walk past me as though I am invisible." Many experience this sense of invisibility. It may be someone who does a menial job, someone who feels anonymous in our church, someone who always stands alone at social gatherings, or someone who begs on the street corner for food. Often, the invisible ones are people written off by our society as no longer productive or useful. The forgotten elderly, the victims of mental illness, those with disabilities, the incurably ill, the beggars—they are "invisible" persons who come immediately to mind. They yearn for the blessing that comes from truly being seen.

Learning to see someone in this way does not come easily. First, we need to learn to look beyond ourselves. Our eyes need to be opened so that we are not always thinking of our own needs and desires. Frequently we focus only on what we are thinking and feeling. How often do we ask ourselves, *Is there anyone here who feels invisible and alone, someone whom I truly need to see?* Without this awareness of others, we will not become channels of God's blessing.

Second, we need to slow down. Those who are always in a hurry seldom have time to see the people in front of them. When our lives move quickly like a fast train, everything becomes a blur, including those around us. We cannot bring blessings to persons who are passing blurs! In our hurry, they are much more likely to feel cursed by us. Intentionally eliminating hurry from our lives frees us to see beyond appearances and see others through the eyes of our Divine Friend. When we see people in this way, we bring blessing to all who cross our path.

Who might be invisible in our presence? If we are parents, it may be our children. If we are married, it may be our partner. If we are managers, it may be someone in our department. If we are pastors, it may be a member in the congregation. If we are teachers, it may be a student. If we are doctors, it may be a patient. If we are coaches, it may be someone on our team. The list of possibilities goes on. To really see someone, whether a loved one or a complete stranger, is to give that person a special blessing.

friendship exercise

Reflect on the current state of your spiritual eyesight. Here are some questions that can help your evaluation. Is my seeing limited by a person's outward appearance? Am I always in a hurry? Do I make up my mind up quickly about those I meet? Am I more loving and accepting toward those who look affluent and successful?

If you answered one or more of those questions in the affirmative, I invite you to pray a one-sentence prayer that I often pray, *Lord Jesus, please help me to see each person today as a person of infinite value and immense worth.* When you embody this prayer, your life will offer blessing to those around you.

The Blessing of Presence

Though we discussed the importance of seeing others, we must go beyond that act in order to bless others. We must learn to be present. What does that mean? Being present involves letting go of our constant preoccupations, immersing ourselves in the here and now, and giving ourselves to whomever or whatever is in front of us at the moment. Presence goes far beyond being physically present. It means engaging the other person with all our heart, our mind, our soul, and our strength. This is one of the greatest blessings we can give to those around us. Often when I am asked how we can bless those going through difficult times, I respond, "With your presence." Be all there!

However, being present in this focused way can be hard. I remember answering "present" to the teacher who called my name even when my mind was far away. I was physically present, but inwardly I had migrated to another place. Sometimes I sense that same lack of presence in the congregation when I preach. Physically, bodies are in the pews; people even look in my direction. But I can tell from the glazed look in their eyes that their hearts and minds are elsewhere. It is a massive challenge to "be all there" for another person.

When we are truly present with others, we bless them. We bless them more than we know when we offer the gift of our undivided and listening attention. We help them to know that they matter, that their lives are valuable, and that they are infinitely precious to God. I have little doubt that this is what Jesus' presence meant to those around him. He always seemed to be present to those around him, whoever they were or whatever they had done. No wonder his life was a continuous and consistent source of blessing.

If we truly want to bless others, helpful action will follow our presence with them—not the other way around. Sometimes we rush in too quickly with what we believe will assist another person. Gerald May, one of my favorite authors, suggests that we can become addicted to being helpful rather than taking the time to be lovingly present. With tongue in cheek, he classifies some of us by our habits of helpfulness in a lighthearted list. We can probably identify our own particular "helpfulness habit" that ironically keeps us from being truly present.

There is the person who always wants to get you to talk about your troubles. I'll call this person the *empathophile*; it is someone who seems convinced that everything can be made better by sharing. "Come over here, and tell me all about it."

I myself am a Technofixer. My immediate impulse is to get into your situation with my do-it-yourself repair kit. "Let me call your lawyer for you." "I know a place where you can get a low-interest loan." "Have you tried counting sheep?"

Then there's the Nuzzlecuddler. There is no problem so great that can't be made better with a hug. Nuzzlecuddlers seldom say much; they just come at you with open arms and a silly smile. They are my favorites; I want at least one around whenever I am in trouble (or even when I'm not).

I also love Grub Fairies. No matter what the trouble is, they'll fix you something to eat. They are very straightforward, saying nothing about your problem, just, "I brought you a pie." There is a rare and wonderful subspecies called the Chocolate Grub Fairy. With a Chocolate Grub Fairy and a Nuzzlecuddler by my side, I think I could endure anything.

And of course there's the Portable Shoulder: they pull you to them and say, "Just let it all out."

The Theological Psychotic smiles reassuringly and then hits you with, "It's all God's will."[2]

We may find that each of these responses, with the exception of the "Theological Psychotic," is helpful at times, but the challenge of real love ultimately lies in being present. Being present to others enables us to be with them before rushing into one of our automatic "helpful" responses. We can take time to discern a helpful response and when to offer it. Presence always precedes action if we want to bless others.

friendship exercise

For the next twenty-four hours try to become aware of your automatic habits of helpfulness—the usual ways you try help people. Make a conscious effort, asking God for help, to stop doing them. Instead, give yourself more space between being present with someone and trying to help them. This change may feel a bit awkward. In this space, seek to discern love's response. Perhaps you are being invited to pray, remain silent, or put a hand on a shoulder. Consider using new and different ways of being helpful to others.

The Blessing of Words

Finally, we bless others with our words. "To bless," in Latin, is *benedicere*, which literally translates as "speaking good." This means affirming others and making them aware of our delight in being with them. It means wanting good things for them and asking God to be with them in a special way. Words of blessing project goodness into the lives of others with the help of God. Certainly all these meanings are implied in the great benediction that Aaron speaks over the people of Israel: "The LORD bless you and keep you; the LORD make his face to shine upon you, and be gracious to you; the LORD lift up his countenance upon you, and give you peace" (Num. 6:24-26).

Henri J. M. Nouwen relates a moving example of this kind of blessing in his book *Life of the Beloved: Spiritual Living in a Secular World*. Janet, a member of the L'Arche Daybreak community where Nouwen ministered, asks him for a blessing. Almost without thinking, Nouwen traces the sign of the cross on her forehead with his thumb, but Janet protests, asking for a "real blessing." So he promises her that he will try again that night at their prayer service.

Later in the evening when Nouwen and Janet are sitting with the other members of the community, Nouwen shares Janet's request for a blessing. As soon as he mentions this, she stands up, walks toward him, and buries her head on his chest. As they hold each other, he begins to speak good over her life. "Janet, I want you to know that you are God's Beloved Daughter. You are precious in God's eyes. Your beautiful smile, your kindness to the people in your house and all the good things you do show us what a beautiful human being you are. I know you feel a little low these days and that there is some sadness in your heart, but I want you to remember who you are: a very special person, deeply loved by God and all the people who are here with you."[3]

As Nouwen speaks these words, Janet raises her head and looks at him. Her smile conveys that she has received his blessing. Afterward, nearly all the other community members come forward expressing the same desire to be blessed. Finally, one of the assistants, a young university student, raises his hand and asks for a blessing too. Nouwen puts his arms around him and says, "John, it is so good that you are here. You are God's Beloved Son. Your presence is a joy for all of us. When things are hard and life is burdensome, always remember that you are loved with an everlasting love."[4] As John receives this blessing, he offers Nouwen his sincere thanks.

As we reflect on this moment between the priest and his little congregation, we see more clearly what it means to bless others with our words. There are no magical formulas or correct words to say. If there were, we would run the risk of empty repetition and vain superstition. We simply use whatever words we think appropriate to speak good into another person's life. We may use the traditional

"Peace be with you," or we could offer a more spontaneous "I am so grateful for you" or "May you always know you are God's beloved." Words like these, spoken with confident faith in the God who blesses, can transmit immeasurable blessing into the lives of those around us, especially when they come from a real and genuine place inside us.

Words of blessing can be spoken to everyone. Sadly, we sometimes exclude or overlook certain people. We may take those closest to us for granted and forget to express our appreciation and gratitude for their lives. Sometimes we withhold blessing from people who have hurt us, forgetting Jesus' words about blessing those who curse us. Though we often want to curse individuals who are involved in murders, child abuse, hijacking incidents, and other criminal activities, perhaps we could bless them by saying, "Lord, bless that person with true remorse and repentance."

friendship exercise

Make tomorrow a "blessing day." Ask God early in the day to fill your heart with God's love for all those you meet. Resolve to extend a blessing to each person you encounter, beginning with those closest to you. You don't have to say, "God bless you" to everyone. Your blessing may be a spontaneous word of encouragement, an inwardly whispered prayer asking that God's presence be real and felt, or a comment like "I am so glad that you are alive." Speak a blessing in faith that God will use your words to bless others. Reflect on your experience at the end of the day, and pay special attention to what effect your practice had on your friendship with God.

As Jesus' friends we are called to live as children of our heavenly Parent who "makes his sun rise on the evil and on the good, and sends rain on the righteous and on the unrighteous" (Matt. 5:45). Just as it is the sun's nature to always shine, so too is it God's nature to love this world and bless everyone in it. Like Abraham, we are called to be agents of God's blessing, especially to those who feel cursed. Wouldn't it be wonderful if we were known in a world of cursing as sources of blessing? This is part of what it means to live in friendship with God and to make God's dream real in our world today.

A CLOSING INVITATION

Let me state again the offer at the heart of the gospel: God wants to be our intimate friend. Through the life, death, resurrection, and ascension of Jesus Christ, God offers us the following assurance:

> I have desired you into being for the sake of friendship. This is why you are here. I am closer to you than you will ever be able to imagine. If you accept my outstretched hand, we can begin to grow an intimate friendship. I want to get to know you, to reveal myself to you, and to live in communion with you. In your moments of failure and sin, let the cross always remind you that I will never stop desiring your friendship. Nothing can ever extinguish the flame of my longing for friendship with every human being.
>
> As your friend, I want us to work together as partners in making my dream real in this world. I hope and dream that all people will live in friendship with me and with one another. Do not be put off by the bigness of this calling. Begin where you find yourself. Love those closest to you. See your neighbor as someone with whom I also want to be friends. Bless all who cross your path with the blessing you have received from me. Worship regularly with my community of friends, immerse yourself together in the biblical story, and welcome everyone to my table.

Above all, know that you will never be alone. Face your fears and share them with me. When you weep, I will weep with you. When you rejoice, I will rejoice with you. In your darkness and suffering, remember I am constantly seeking to bring about the hope of life and resurrection. Nothing—not even death—can ever separate you from my love. Indeed, we shall be friends forever.

NOTES

Foreword

1. James Martin, SJ, *The Jesuit Guide to (Almost) Everything: A Spirituality for Real Life* (San Francisco: HarperOne, 2010), 115.

1   Living beyond Loneliness

1. Alex Ferguson, *Alex Ferguson: My Autobiography* (London: Hodder & Stoughton, 2013), 38.
2. Parker Palmer, *Let Your Life Speak: Listening for the Voice of Vocation* (San Francisco: Jossey-Bass, 2000), 63–4.
3. Dallas Willard, *In Search of Guidance: Developing a Conversational Relationship with God* (New York: HarperCollins, 1993), 36. (This book has been reissued under the title *Hearing God* by InterVarsity Press, 1999.)

2   God's Passionate Longing for Friendship

1. William A. Barry, SJ explores this idea of our "default image of God" in chapter 14 of *Here's My Heart, Here's My Hand: Living Fully in Friendship with God* (Chicago: Loyola Press, 2009).
2. Jean Vanier, *Drawn into the Mystery of Jesus through the Gospel of John,* (Toronto, ON: Novalis, 2004), 272.
3. Ibid., 268.

3 Getting to Know Our Friend

1. Rowan Williams, *Tokens of Trust: An Introduction to Christian Belief* (London: Canterbury Press Norwich, 2007), 73–5.
2. Adapted from the dedication of Joseph F. Girzone's book *Never Alone: A Personal Way to God* (Dublin, Ireland: Gill & Macmillan Ltd., 1994).

4 Understanding Prayer as Deepening Friendship

1. M. Basil Pennington, *Challenges in Prayer*, (New York: Health Policy Advisory Center, 1982), 23.
2. The best book on this subject is Dallas Willard's *Hearing God: Developing a Conversational Relationship with God* (Downers Grove, IL: InterVarsity Press, 1999).
3. Martin, *The Jesuit Guide*, 126.

5 Looking Outward Together

1. William A. Barry, SJ, *Changed Heart, Changed World: The Transforming Freedom of Friendship with God* (Chicago: Loyola Press, 2011), 19.
2. Dallas Willard, *The Divine Conspiracy: Rediscovering Our Hidden Life in God* (San Francisco: HarperSanFrancisco, 1998), 243.

6 Exploring Our Friend's Address Book

1. Leslie D. Weatherhead, *The Transforming Friendship: A Book About Jesus and Ourselves* (Nashville, TN: Abingdon Press, 1990), 44-5.

7 Discerning What Our Friend Wants Us to Do

1. Willard, *In Search of Guidance*, xii–xiii.

8 Facing Our Fears with Our Friend

1. David G. Benner, *Surrender to Love: Discovering the Heart of Christian Spirituality* (Downers Grove, IL: InterVarsity Press, 2003), 50.

2. William A. Barry, SJ, *God's Passionate Desire* (Chicago: Loyola Press, 2008), 65.

9 Asking Our Friend the Hardest Question

1. William Barclay, *Testament of Faith* (Oxford, England: A. R. Mowbray & Co. Ltd., 1975), 45.
2. Ibid., 46.

10 Blessing Others as Our Friend Has Blessed Us

1. Ronald Rolheiser, *Sacred Fire: A Vision for a Deeper Human and Christian Maturity* (New York: Image, 2014), 225.
2. Gerald G. May, *The Awakened Heart: Living Beyond Addiction* (New York: HarperCollins Publishers, 1991), 238.
3. Henri J. M. Nouwen, *Life of the Beloved: Spiritual Living in a Secular World* (New York: Crossroad Publishing Company, 1992), 58.
4. Ibid., 59.